THE CLINICAL PERSPECTIVE IN FIELDWORK

EDGAR H. SCHEIN
Massachusetts Institute of Technology

Qualitative Research Methods,
Volume 5

SAGE PUBLICATIONS
The Publishers of Professional Social Science
Newbury Park   Beverly Hills   London   New Delhi

Printed in the United States of America

For information address:

SAGE Publications, Inc.
2111 West Hillcrest Drive
Newbury Park, California 91320

SAGE Publications Inc.   SAGE Publications Ltd.
275 South Beverly Drive   28 Banner Street
Beverly Hills   London EC1Y 8QE
California 90212   England

SAGE PUBLICATIONS India Pvt. Ltd.
M-32 Market
Greater Kailash I
New Delhi 110 048 India

International Standard Book Number 0-8039-2975-7
0-8039-2976-5 (pbk)

Library of Congress Catalog Card No. 87-42733

FIRST PRINTING

When citing a university paper, please use the proper form. Remember to cite the correct
Sage University Paper series title and include the paper number. One of the following
formats can be adapted (depending on the style manual used):

(1) IVERSEN, GUDMUND R. and NORPOTH, HELMUT (1976) "Analysis of
Variance." Sage University Paper series on Quantitative Applications in the Social
Sciences, 07-001. Beverly Hills: Sage Pubns.

OR

(2) Iversen, Gudmund R. and Norpoth, Helmut. 1976. *Analysis of Variance.* Sage
University Paper series on Quantitative Applications in the Social Sciences, series no.
07-001. Beverly Hills: Sage Pubns.

CONTENTS

EDITORS' INTRODUCTION

Problem-solving research undertaken at the request of others has a long history in the social sciences and fieldwork is a familiar method accompanying many of these change-oriented studies. It is, however, fieldwork of a strategic and restricted sort since it is accomplished by invitation only and the mark of its success is not the advancement of science, social theory, or general knowledge per se, but the provision of practical, acknowledged, here-and-now aid to those who sponsor the research. Edgar Schein takes up the pursuit of these goals from a clinical perspective in this fifth monograph of the Qualitative Research Methods Series. At issue is what it means to take an active, diagnostic, and curative stance in the field. A process model of research is outlined in this book whereby the outsider, companion-friend, ethnographic role for the fieldworker is contrasted to and, in some instances, displaced by the insider, consultant-collaborator, clinical role. Of special interest is that the clinician, unlike the ethnographer, is welcome in the halls, meeting rooms, and corner offices occupied by those in high position and, thus, can help remove some of the mystery of why the powerful act as they do. The price paid for such access is, of course, the researcher's willingness to work toward the solution of client-defined problems. But, as Professor Schein makes clear, competent clinical work in organizational settings is not a hierarchically defined change effort with fieldwork-for-a-fee tacked on to evaluate the efforts; but, competent clinical fieldwork demands a long-term, open-ended, give-and-take commitment to bringing about organizational change, a process that inevitably involves shifts in both the client's and clinician's point of view.

John Van Maanen
Peter K. Manning
Marc L. Miller

5

PREFACE

This book is something of an experiment. I have been struck for some time by the difficulty of figuring out what "really" goes on in groups, organizations, and human systems in general. I have also been struck by the gap that exists between our traditional "scientific" knowledge of such matters, what we find in our scholarly journals of social and organizational psychology, on the one hand, and what we "know" from our own experience as members of organizations, as managers, and as helpers and consultants, on the other hand.

This more immediate knowledge has not gained the respectability it deserves and we have not sufficiently legitimized the gathering of such knowledge. This book is an effort to close that gap somewhat—to show that we can know from our immediate experience, especially when we are in helping and consulting roles, and to argue that this "clinical" method or perspective, as I will call it, has a legitimate place in doing research on individuals, groups, and organizations.

My intended audience is broad. I think the scholar of human systems must have at least an awareness of the issues brought out here. The consultant, helper, clinician may find that the ideas presented here will sharpen his or her thinking about the clinical role and its potential. Practicing managers and members of organizations can benefit from seeing how they can use their own clinical and helping roles vis-à-vis their superiors, peers, and subordinates, and also obtain some insight into how to *be* a client should they find themselves in that role.

This book also provides an opportunity to repay some intellectual debts that go back 30 years or more. I first became exposed to clinical methods because the Harvard Social Relations Department Ph.D. program required some form of internships from all of its students. I spent a year at the Walter Reed Army Hospital learning to give tests and to observe how a psychiatric ward operated.

In my subsequent first job at the Walter Reed Army Institute of Research I benefited immensely from the wisdom and insight of David

Rioch, my then boss and mentor. He exemplified perfectly the clinician whose goal was to add to knowledge, and his ability to draw out of clinical experience has always been a model for me. During my four years at Walter Reed I became involved with the exchange of prisoners of war following the Korean conflict and found myself in the twin role of researcher and clinician as we attempted both to understand and to help repatriates coming out of North Korean prison camps and subsequently out of Chinese mainland prisons (Schein, 1956, 1961).

After my stint in the Army I began my academic career at MIT under the mentorship of Douglas McGregor. His seminal insights (McGregor, 1960) were based on his own formal research, his stint as President of Antioch College, and his exposure to the new action research approaches being developed by Kurt Lewin and his followers. Doug suggested that I might benefit from exposure to a training group experience at Bethel, Maine, where the National Training Laboratories group was working out the technology of experiential methods for leadership and group training based on Lewin's original concepts and experiments. I discovered in my first direct group experience in 1957 that I learned far more about groups by being in one as an observer and participant, than I ever had attempting to study groups in the laboratory.

I became an apprentice staff member and eventually a regular staff member at workshops and spent some 15 to 20 years practicing the twin role of group facilitator and student of group behavior. During those years, my exposure to the architects of the whole experiential learning method—Lee Bradford, Ken Benne, Richard Beckhard, Ron Lippitt, and, of course, Doug McGregor —deepened my interest in the kind of knowledge that one obtains during the process of teaching and helping people.

My own consulting experience was greatly enriched by the close contact I had with Doug McGregor and Dick Beckhard, and my theoretical understanding of the interplay between clinical work and research was further enhanced by getting to know members of the Tavistock Institute, particularly Harold Bridger and Eric Trist. Similar insights came from association over the years with Harry Levinson, particularly during the year that he taught at MIT in the 1960s.

The persons who have most influenced my thinking about this area in recent times are Lotte Bailyn, John Van Maanen, and Gideon Kunda. Our joint interest in a clinical seminar, which was co-led by Gideon and me, and our running intellectual debate about the "best" way to do research on human systems has immeasurably enriched my thinking about this area. We have found that there is no one best way, and that what we must strive for is a deeper understanding of each of the many ways to further our knowledge of human systems.

The members of the seminar who helped greatly to clarify these issues were Lotte Bailyn, Steve Barley, Barbara Bigelow, John Chillingarian, Deborah Dougherty, Anna Maria Garden, Dale Goodhue, Deborah Kolb, Gideon Kunda, Elliott Levinson, Tom Malone, Jack Rockart, John Van Maanen, and Gordon Walker.

Last but certainly not least, I must acknowledge all of the clients who have provided the setting in which to pursue this inquiry. For reasons of privacy they must remain anonymous but their help is enormously appreciated.

As usual the supportive environment provided by my wife, and the growing interest in these matters on the part of my children who are entering careers that involve both research and clinical work has helped immensely to get this work out. I appreciate their support and stimulation.

Edgar H. Schein
Cambridge, MA
September, 1986

THE CLINICAL PERSPECTIVE IN FIELDWORK

EDGAR H. SCHEIN
Massachusetts Institute of Technology

1. DISCOVERING THE CLINICAL PERSPECTIVE

The purpose of this monograph is to make explicit some of the assumptions and methodologies of what I am calling here the *clinical* perspective or model, and to contrast these with other approaches to data gathering and analysis, especially the ethnographic approach. I believe that the clinician starts with a different mind-set, a different set of assumptions about how one can and should work with and study people, groups, communities, and organizations, what I will broadly label *living human systems.* I will argue that these assumptions have not only far reaching consequences for the investigator's moment to moment behavior, but also for the kind of data that will be revealed about the human system and its actors.

What do I mean by clinical? For purposes of this essay I will mean those helping professionals who get involved with individuals, groups, communities, or organizations in a "helping role." This would include clinical and counseling psychologists, psychiatrists, social workers, organization development consultants, process consultants, and others who work explicitly with human systems. I refer to trained professionals, not amateurs, so there is implied in my use of the concept of the "clinical perspective" the notion that the person has been educated and trained to

11

take this perspective. It is not automatic. The training can come from a variety of fields such as psychology, education, medicine, applied sociology, and applied anthropology. In focusing on this perspective I am not trying to distinguish different academic disciplines, but rather the stance that the clinical practitioners within a discipline take vis-à-vis others in that or related disciplines.

Most of my examples will be drawn from my practice as a process consultant (Schein, 1969, 1987). My focus will be on the perspective I take toward this kind of work, not the day to day routine of how such work is done nor the particular skills required to do it. Those issues are covered in detail in my two books on process consultation.

I will not spend much time distinguishing the clinical from the *experimental* model because that distinction is fairly obvious and well documented. It is more important to distinguish the clinical from the ethnographic model because on the surface these resemble each other. In both models the investigator attempts to enter the system in a somewhat quiet unobtrusive manner and is working "in the field" rather than in the controlled environment of the "laboratory."

There has also been a tendency, particularly among organizational researchers, to lump clinical and ethnographic methods together under the broader label of *qualitative* research, a term that does little to help us sort out what the essential characteristics are of the many different ways of gathering data that are not primarily quantitative or experimental. As I will try to show, the distinction between clinical and ethnographic may have more profound consequences than whether the inquiry is conducted quantitatively or qualitatively.

Some Historical Perspective

The idea of this book originated in a meeting of teachers of organizational psychology and sociology held at the Harvard Business School in 1983. We listened to some general lectures on the pressing research problems in our field, and then got together in small groups to explore these research issues in greater depth.

At one point, a member of the group I was attending raised the question of how research results enter our classroom teaching. One of us volunteered that what we relied on for illustrations in the classroom came much more from what we learned as consultants or practitioners than what we found in our professional journals. At some level we trusted such data more than what was revealed by the seemingly more scientific methods of our published research.

This rather "shocking revelation" was then checked with other members of the conference and we found, to our surprise, that *almost all of us had the same experience.* The data we really believed in and used in the classroom came from our personal experiences in organizations. What was in our journals might spark theoretical insights, might confirm what we learned "in the field," and might occasionally enrich our teaching, but did not serve as the basic data we relied on. Clearly what we trusted and believed in as what "really goes on" in organizations came from our practical experience, especially those experiences where we were functioning as helpers and consultants, where we were, in effect, operating as clinicians, not researchers in the traditional model.

We also confessed that what we read in our journals often was perceived by us and by our students as not having the "ring of truth" to it. It seemed as if many of our colleagues who relied solely on experimental and survey research somehow did not seem to "understand" organizational realities in the manner in which those of us who did consulting and field research believed we did. It was almost as if there were two separate camps of researchers—(1) those who relied strictly on positivistic empirical experimental and survey research, and who felt no particular need to immerse themselves in organizational "realities," and (2) those who relied more on the knowledge gained in consulting experiences and in various kinds of fieldwork driven more by sociological and anthropological research models.

In thinking about this experience and the acknowledgment that so many of us had a similar view of what we relied on in the classroom made me more conscious of the distinction between the different categories of knowledge that can be obtained by different methods. The distinction between *qualitative* and *quantitative* was being widely explored already, but within the qualitative domain, it seemed to me there were some major further distinctions that were being overlooked by us, having to do with the meaning of the word "clinical."

In many accounts of qualitative research, the journalistic, ethnographic, case analysis, fieldwork, and clinical approaches were all lumped together. No clear distinction was being made between these various approaches and what I will develop here as the "clinical" perspective. In fact, as we will see, the best way to expound what I see to be the clinical perspective is to contrast it sharply with the ethnographic model of research. These two models are often lumped together, yet, as I will argue, *they are almost totally different in the kind of insight and knowledge that they generate, in the assumptions upon which they rest, and in what they require of the researcher.*

The conclusion I will reach is that both perspectives are ultimately necessary to understand fully what goes on in groups, communities, and organizations, but only by understanding the differences in the perspectives can we grasp fully what is meant by saying that we need *both* perspectives.

The 1984 MIT Clinical Seminar. In order to explore these issues, a number (10 to 15) of faculty and graduate students at the Sloan School created a "clinical seminar." Our goal was to bring live case material into the seminar and to discuss together how our "on-line" experience could be converted into credible, reliable research data. How did we each manage this transition in our own head, and how could we communicate our insights to colleagues?

We took turns presenting material either from our ethnographic, field interview, or consulting projects. Gideon Kunda, one of our advanced Ph.D. students with clinical and group experience, served as coleader with me. The objective was to listen to a presentation and then together decipher the significance of what the presenter had learned. We also wanted to be able to explore the revealed data without recourse to any particular formal theory or model, to let the data lead us, so to speak, and, to this end, encouraged faculty and students from widely different disciplines to attend if they were interested. These seemed to be worthwhile goals and were enthusiastically embraced by all members who attended the first few meetings.

Problems in the seminar. My observation of the first six to eight weeks of the seminar was that the seminar itself was so governed by traditional academic norms that we had difficulty being helpful to each other in achieving our stated goals of gaining some mutual understanding and insights. We found ourselves "interrogating" the presenter, competing with each other for airtime, arguing with each other about the validity of ideas presented, and generally behaving in a manner that I labeled as "aggressive," though some members aggressively denied that there was any aggression present. For many, the level of discourse seemed normal to the situation, but one could not escape the observation that we had difficulty maintaining a coherent thread through any given seminar, could not agree on any conclusions, and generally were frustrated that things were not working out better.

A poem by Jim March says it better than any description I could offer of what many of us began to experience:

One More Time

I am older
And have buried my instinct
For the delicate destruction
Of intellectual intercourse
In the clutter
Of my wrinkles.

Still,
I hear your challenge
And accept it
As the way things ought to be.

Arguments
Are the arenas
In which educated men
Establish their right
To imagine themselves
Alive.

You choose the domain:
    Philosophy.
    Methodology.
    Theory.
    Politics.
And you speak first.

Choose carefully
And speak smart.

Because

If I can,

I will

Chop up your ideas

Stuff them into an old condom

And hang them in my trophy room.

J.G. March
Academic Notes, 1974, p. 72

My own recollections of a typical seminar were as follows. A previously designated presenter would attempt to tell a story about himself or herself, often with a question on which he or she wanted some *help* from the group. We usually allowed the person 15 minutes or less before we began to interrupt with questions of clarification, rhetorical questions that implied the listener already had a theory of what was going on, challenges of what the protagonist had done, skepticism about the protagonist's own interpretation of what might have been going on, arguments among members of the seminar about interpretations of the presented material, lectures to each other about correct and incorrect points of view toward research, advice on how to conduct oneself in the field, and generally competitive behavior of the kind one sees in any newly formed group.

I found myself dropping out of the role of seminar leader into the role of group trainer, yet whenever I attempted to intervene around group process issues, the group became polarized between the contingent that saw "here-and-now" process as relevant to what the seminar's purposes were and the contingent that saw the competitive debate as the only constructive worthwhile way to proceed.

I found all of this paradoxical because the essence of the clinical method as I saw it was to draw out of the client "deeper" levels of data that could be obtained only by intensive listening and the creation of a psychologically safe and supportive environment (Schein, 1969, 1987). I was operating on the assumption that the presenter could not fully reveal what he or she had learned in the field unless we guaranteed a climate in which such learning would be treated with respect and support. If we made each other insecure and defensive, we would force presentations that were staged for the traditional academic forum rather than for the kind of exploration we were seeking.

Furthermore, it struck me that if we could not create such an environment for ourselves, for our own "clients" in the seminar, our designated presenters, how could we understand the potential of the clinical method out in the field? We had to be clinical toward each other if we were to witness what could be done with the method. But for many members of the seminar that clearly lay outside the psychological contract as they saw it, or they did not perceive the incongruity as I saw it.

My further dilemma was that we were not only failing to be supportive, but were actually behaving aggressively and insensitively toward each other. The protagonist would often get successive unconnected questions from as many as five or six members of the seminar, none of whom seemed to notice the growing distress of the protagonist as he or she attempted to deal with unconnected issues flying in from all sides.

To complicate matters even further, the fact that there were senior faculty, junior faculty, and various levels of graduate students in the seminar introduced power and authority issues that often seemed to get in the way of communication. But by far the most frustrating aspect to me was the inability to get seminar members to "see" the level of aggressiveness, competitiveness, and insensitivity we were displaying, regardless of the dynamic roots of such behavior. It was not my goal to turn the seminar into a sensitivity training group, but it did seem to me that the processes we were actually experiencing gave us an important clue as to the essence of the clinical perspective.

I was, therefore, determined to influence the group's behavior toward more of an "inquiry" model and away from an academic debate model so that we could learn from the process of dealing with each other something about what clinicians learn when they deal with their clients. In other words, because the seminar seemed to be operating on the "traditional" academic discourse model of building scientific truth through an advocacy and disproof paradigm, we were actually cutting off our own opportunity to explore the clinical paradigm.

Changing the climate through a new structure. Several of us who observed this behavior, particularly Gideon Kunda, Lotte Bailyn, and I, decided that we needed to structure the situation differently to stimulate insight into what was going on. We had to find a mechanism to let group members see for themselves what the advocacy and confrontive paradigm led to, as a way of exploring other possible data-gathering paradigms. In particular, if the clinical perspective could be revealed and assessed only if we learned to listen to each other intensely and supportively, then we needed a seminar structure that would encourage such behavior and monitor us if we again became too confrontive and competitive. Over a period of weeks we evolved and "sold" the following alternative seminar structure to accomplish these goals.

(1) A single presenter would be given the floor for as many hours as would be needed (the seminar usually lasted 2 to 3 hours and this ensured that the presenter would feel that he or she could get his or her whole story out).

(2) One member of the seminar would be designated as the interviewer to bring out the presenter's case, and this person would be the only one allowed to speak for the first 30 or so minutes (this ensured some continuity and focus in how the data were revealed and provided, over a period of weeks, some practice in clinical interviewing for different seminar members).

(3) Other seminar members could ask questions and enter the discussion only after the formal interview of 30 minutes was over (this rule enforced listening and provided all of us some practice in listening).

(4) The interview and the subsequent discussion by the total seminar would be videotaped (having the interview on tape would make it possible to reconstruct in detail what kinds of interview techniques were more or less effective in bringing out data, and how the inquiry methods of different members differed from each other; the tapes also provided the interviewees a chance to see how they had presented their story and, thereby, check some of their own biases in reconstructing their field experiences).

(5) As a further exploratory device we had different interviewers take turns interviewing the same protagonist to see whether stylistic variations had an impact on what data were elicited and how the protagonist would respond to different styles (the purpose here was to get on tape different methods for careful reconstruction of different effects and results).

This new structure was designed to deal with some of the realities of the academic culture, and, at the same time, to permit the seminar to surmount the consequences of some of those realities. We assumed that it is natural and desirable to confront ideas competitively and to debate out ideas to see which ones hold up. Any academic group will immediately adopt such behavior unless some specific alternatives are provided.

We also assumed that in any new group everyone will want to establish their role, so some form of competitive task behavior is to be expected and must be allowed for. If people must remain silent for some period of time, one must impose a credible rule and gain acceptance of it. By designating one active interviewer and asking everyone else to be active listeners, and by setting up a process where everyone would later get their turn being an interviewer, we gained acceptance of self-enforced silence for part of each meeting. During the discussion it was, of course, the usual competitive free for all, but we would have it on tape and could assess its consequences.

We also assumed that most academics are not trained in the clinical approach to inquiry so the seminar would have to teach the very method that we wanted to explore. This required a vehicle for learning: (1) the positioning of one of us at a time in a clinical role of "interviewer," (2) the videotaping of our own behavior; and (3) the analysis of different interviewer styles where the interviewer would now become the "client." We had to rely on concrete data (the videotape) inasmuch as our memory of what happened showed consistent disagreements among members, often leading to fruitless debate about what had happened. In other words, the setup had to teach interviewing and active listening skills, and had to do so in a face-preserving manner inasmuch as no one wanted to admit lack of skill in these areas.

The method worked. Not only did the climate change dramatically, but we began to see almost immediately how our own interviewing styles, our methods of asking questions, and our theories of what was going on influenced the kind of data we drew out of our presenters. We could see how skill issues, style issues, and theory issues influenced the actual data that were revealed, and those insights permitted us to extrapolate these same issues into our various field settings.

For example, we found that what the protagonist actually remembered as historical events in a given situation that he or she was describing varied as a function of whether the interviewer was testing a hypothesis and subtly "leading the witness" or was interviewing "nondirectively" providing the interviewee the opportunity to project their own hypotheses into the situation. Both methods produced useful data, but they were very different data.

The need for constructs. One of the issues that plagued us throughout the seminar was the lack of theoretical constructs on which we could agree. We used words like quantitative and qualitative differently, we misunderstood each other's research paradigms, often leading to fruitless debates, and, most of all, from my point of view, we had no common understanding of what I meant by the "clinical" perspective or method. Apart from discovering together what the clinical perspective meant in the seminar context, there was an obvious need to articulate in more theoretical and formal terms what I meant, and what my assumptions were.

I had been interested in this topic and had constructed an outline for a talk that focused especially on the contrast between clinical and ethnographic research. It seemed to me that too many so-called "qualitative" methods were being lumped together under a broad clinical/ethnographic umbrella. This outline provided the basic structure for the next several chapters. By sharpening the contrast between clinical and ethnographic, I hope to create a vehicle for forcing clarity about what is meant by "clinical."

Contrast Between Ethnographic and Clinical as a Heuristic Device

In choosing to elucidate the clinical perspective by contrasting it as much as possible with the ethnographic I am focusing my attention on the models as pure types, not necessarily how they actually work out in practice. Many of the things I will attribute to each model will strike the practitioner as exaggerations, and it will be immediately noted that in practice the two models not only have many subvarieties but that they blend into each other in complex ways.

However, I have found that it is crucial for the person in the field, that is, working in an organization with members of that organization, to be very clear at all times whether he or she is operating in the *general role* of a clinician or in the *general role* of an ethnographer, even if the daily behavior involves a complex blending of these roles. The perspective that the inquirer takes toward the organization member, toward the data, and toward the inquiry process itself will be very different according to his or her self-perceived role, as I will try to show.

Self insight into one's role and the implied self management become critical when choices have to be made between what is best for the client organization and what is best for the inquirer. The organization member will typically be unaware of these choices, so it is the clinician/ethnographer who must make them on the basis of professional standards that are ethical and protect various constituencies in the organization. As we will see, how these choices are made differs greatly depending upon whether one sees oneself in the clinician or ethnographer role.

The use of sharp contrast in defining the roles should aid the reader in thinking through the various professional and ethical issues that may be involved in working with human systems. The principle of informed consent that has been advocated as a way of protecting unsuspecting "subjects" from insensitive or malicious researchers works only if the subject knows what is really going on; that is, what he or she is consenting to. When a clinician or an ethnographer enters an organization, do the members of that organization know enough to make an informed consent choice? In my experience they do not, and it falls, therefore, to the person entering the organization to apply initially the appropriate professional standards unilaterally, and to educate the client as quickly as possible to what they have committed themselves.

The Issue of Professionalism and Ethics

I referred above to professional standards and the need for the person entering the organization to be accountable for those standards. This position derives from the assumption that professional ethics and standards ultimately revolve around the issue of client vulnerability (Schein, 1966, 1972). If the client or research subject can understand what the professional is doing and what its consequences will be, then the principle of "caveat emptor," or buyer beware, makes sense. But to the extent that the buyer, subject, or client either does not know enough or is not capable of comprehending the implications of the knowledge, the professional must be held accountable for the welfare of the other.

It is not clear to me that this issue is raised in the same way in the education of a clinician and ethnographer. The formally educated clinician is trained to think in terms of protecting the client from unscrupulous, wasteful, or harmful treatments, and is made aware of the necessity to create a supportive environment in order to elucidate whatever information is needed to make a good diagnosis on the basis of which to give a valid and helpful prescription. If the clinician is working from a process consultation model (Schein, 1969, 1987) he or she is further enjoined to learn how to manage the relationship to enhance the client's ability to learn to continue to solve his or her own problems. Part of being truly professional in that context is to avoid creating too much dependency on the part of the client. The crucial point is that the clinical attitude or role of wanting to help somebody does not guarantee that the helper has the professional training, skills, and sense of responsibility to provide the help. The clinical *method,* therefore, implies a high degree of training and experience in addition to a desire to be helpful.

The professional ethics of the ethnographer have much more to do with how to obtain valid information without influencing or disturbing the system being studied any more than is necessary. One should learn about the culture without changing it too much, so the investigator must make himself or herself as much a part of the scene as possible, and must not intervene in ways that would knowingly and deliberately perturb and change the system. Typically, the ultimate goal is to obtain valid data for "science," not to change, help, or in other ways influence the system being studied.

The ability to become an unobtrusive participant observer also requires a high degree of formal education, training, and professional responsibility. Ethnographers are not supposed to become missionaries or consultants, but the kind of training and the kind of responsibility they must exercise are quite different because their "clients" are ultimately the scholarly community. They must produce some version of "truth" without changing too much that which they have studied.

The Plan for This Book

I will elucidate the contrasts by raising a series of fundamental questions about the ethnographer/clinician versus subject/client relationship, and explain the essence of the clinical perspective in the context of the answers to these questions. The questions overlap and are at times redundant, as Table 1 shows, but each version of the question will bring out some unique and important features of the clinical-ethnographic contrast. I will use the terms *client* and *subject* for convenience, recognizing that these are generic terms that often do not fit the real situation.

The subsequent chapters will deal with these questions or issues and provide illustrative material to show in greater detail what I mean by the clinical perspective, especially its advantages and disadvantages. In Chapter 2 I will explore those questions that elucidate the fundamentally different relationship that exists between clinician vis-à-vis client and ethnographic researcher vis-à-vis the subjects of his study: who initiates and "drives" the process, what implicit models underlie the process, and what kind of psychological contract governs the emerging relationship?

TABLE 1
Diagnostic Questions for Contrasting Clinical
and Ethnographic Methods of Inquiry

I. Focus on the Fundamental Relationship

(1) Who initiates the process of inquiry?
(2) What implicit model of the organization operates?
(3) Whose needs drive the process of inquiry and data gathering?
(4) What is the psychological contract?

II. Focus on the Process in Inquiry and Intervention

(5) What is the conceptual focus of the data gathered?
(6) How are data determined to be scientifically valid?
(7) What are clinical data especially relevant for?

III. Professional/Ethical Issues

(8) How should the investigator be trained to conduct inquiry?
(9) How are clinicians and ethnographers alike?
(10) What are the ethical dilemmas?

In Chapter 3 I will explore the implications for data gathering and data validation. How do clinical and ethnographic methods differ in their process of inquiry, their methods of validating information obtained, and the implications of those methods for intervention into human systems. What kinds of activities do clinicians and ethnographers engage in when they are "in the field" and what are the goals and consequences of such activities?

In Chapter 4 I will explore issues of how data are aggregated, written up, cleared with the subject or client, published, and otherwise utilized with an eye to returning to the difficult professional and ethical questions that govern the entire inquiry process in each model. The implications for the professional and ethical training of clinicians and ethnographers will be discussed in this context.

2. HOW THE CLINICAL AND THE ETHNOGRAPHIC RELATIONSHIP DIFFER

Who Initiates the Process of Inquiry?

One of the most central contrasts between the work of the clinician and that of the ethnographer derives from the fact that the client chooses the clinician while the ethnographer chooses the subject group or organization to be studied. The initial "authority" and source for structuring the relationship lies with the client in the clinical relationship and with the ethnographer in the ethnographic relationship.

Clinicians enter an organization or any other human system only if they are requested to do so by someone in the organization or someone acting on the organization's behalf seeking some kind of help. In other words, the initiative in the clinical model is always with the client, even if the person who ultimately ends up in the clinical role has manipulated the situation so that someone in the organization will ask for help.

In contrast, ethnographers typically select an organization as a research site on the basis of their own research or theoretical interests, and must somehow create their own "entry" situation by various stratagems or must take advantage opportunistically of situations that arise. Clinicians are more reactive at the outset in that professional norms militate against the active advertising for and soliciting of business, while ethnographers are more proactive in seeking to enter a system from which something important is to be learned.

Sometimes ethnographers will enter the system unobtrusively by becoming a member of the system or in some other way infiltrating it so as to remain unobtrusive. Clinicians are, by definition, highly visible since they have been asked to come into the organization, though the official reasons given for the entry of consultants and other kinds of helpers may be different from the actual reasons.

As the relationship with the organization develops, it is perfectly possible, indeed quite likely, that the day-to-day roles will merge more and more. Clinicians find opportunities to "wander around" and "observe" in settings that are not initially defined as part of the clinical relationship, and thus are able to gather the kind of data that the ethnographer is seeking. They can even use the clinical relationship to request the opportunity to go out and observe if they and their clients view that as helpful, but the point of reference is always the client's defined needs for help, and the value of the observations is, of course, limited by the clinician's skill in making ethnographic observations.

Ethnographers are likely to be thrust increasingly into clinical roles as they come to be taken for granted and build up trust. They will be asked to give advice, make comments on situations, and actively help to solve problems. They will observe situations that require immediate interventions to keep people from being harmed or messing up, but they will be aware as they are getting involved in these situations that they are in a potential "role conflict" in that they are intervening in the situation above and beyond their own original needs to understand what is going on, and possibly beyond their own level of competence. Some brief examples will highlight these points.

The clinician as ethnographer. Much of my work in the Action Co. (Schein, 1985) was structured around the clinical task of helping the senior executive committee of the company to function better as a work team. I was recruited into this role by the president's administrative assistant and had to discuss the whole project with the president. It was clear to me that I was being evaluated as a potential helper and that the president or others whom I met could have vetoed the project at any time.

In order to get the help that the president felt he needed, he asked me to attend regular weekly staff meetings and to intervene "on line" as I saw problems come up. The initial setting to which I was given access thus was totally specified by the client. However, as the relationship with the Action Co. developed, some of the work was shifted to various other settings in which ethnographic observation became more possible.

For example, the company often conducted intensive two day off-site meetings in which the behavior of the group became much more amenable to intensive observation. Other managers were invited to such meetings so I began to get to know a broader spectrum of people in the company. Opportunities to intervene and be helpful came up whenever the group clearly developed communication or problem-solving difficulties so my observations had to be geared to taking advantage of such opportunities, but much of the time I just listened and noted passively how various members of the group acted and reacted. I took occasional notes but mostly let myself just absorb whatever was happening around the issue of how the group was functioning in the context of my own model of how a group should function.

As I learned later my own model was, in fact, a filter that got in the way of learning some critical things about the culture of this company. As my interventions failed to produce the desired results it became possible to explore my own filters and gradually to learn what assumptions the group was making about itself, how it was perceiving its reality, how it was using language, and, therefore, how I could become more helpful by intervening in a manner more consistent with their culture (Schein, 1985).

One of the key problems that was identified within a few months of my starting to work with the company was the problem of the engineering group's morale. I was asked to interview engineers for purposes of identifying some of the problems and issues that were facing this group. The realities of setting up those interviews were such that I spent a great deal of time hanging around the department where they worked and catching people singly or in groups as the opportunities arose. I also set up structured meetings in private offices, but a great deal of what I did had to be done in the natural work setting.

Interviewing some 75 engineers singly and in groups, meeting with them to review their own data, preparing feedback reports to them and to their managers took approximately six months working one or two days per week in the company. Much of what I observed was just general information about how the company operated, but my focus was on the engineering role, its relationship to other functions, how engineering was managed, and so on, foci that were specified by the senior managers who wanted me to do the interviews.

As I became better known by various members of the company I could enter other departments and simply wander around if I chose to do so. The occasions for such visits were the regular meetings with the executive committees or interviews I had set up to work on various projects. I was perceived as "generally helpful" so I spent two or three days per month in the company over a period of years. The relationship was open-ended in that I indicated a willingness to come to the company "when they needed me for some purpose," but always at their initiative. So there would be long periods where I would not visit at all, and occasional periods where I would get intensely involved in some project.

Other managers invited me to meet with their groups, and I was occasionally asked to give lectures to larger groups that increased my visibility further. My "wandering around" was limited only by my awareness that my presence had symbolic connotations. If I was around a certain area, that could mean that that area was having problems because they were being seen by the "consultant."

As it happened, the culture of the Action Co. was such that people were not particularly threatened by this kind of activity, but in another company in which I worked as a consultant for about five years, the Multi Co. (Schein, 1985), I was absolutely unable to move into any informal settings because defensiveness was so high around being "seen with the consultant." The only meetings I had with people were structured around specific questions or problems that managers wanted to address "with the consultant," and if my contact client asked around about others who might wish to spend some time with me during my quarterly visits, he often encountered blank looks and queries around

"Why would I want to see Ed Schein? I don't have any problems or questions."

Even in the more constrained environment of the Multi Co. many occasions arose where straight observation of what was going on was possible during lunches, during tours of the facilities, during large meetings of the management group where I could observe while awaiting my turn to make my own scheduled presentation, and so on. But I was never left alone and it would not have been possible to wander around without someone immediately accosting me with the question of whom I was looking for. To the extent that I needed ethnographic information about this organization, it had to be dug out of various informants over meals and at other occasions defined as "informal."

As I will try to show later, such observations were useful background data, but the deciphering of critical organizational dynamics required in the end much more than passive observation or even focused interviews. On the other hand, actual incidents that occurred inevitably enriched my diagnostic insight. For example, in the executive dining room of Multi I would sometimes encounter senior managers with whom I had worked, only to have them look right past me and pretend that they did not know me. Such incidents when analyzed with inside informants provided invaluable insights as to how people in Multi felt about their jobs, the company, their peers, and outsiders. Their failing to acknowledge me was highly visible proof of their fear of being seen by their peers as "needing help."

In summary, though the clinical relationship is constantly renegotiated as a function of how helpful it is seen to be, it can last for a long time and thus provide ample opportunities to broaden the base of observation and inquiry. However, I can never afford to forget that the moment I cease to be helpful, the client can terminate the relationship and I cannot make any claim to be allowed to remain in the organization. The ethnographer, in contrast, often must develop a longer-range perspective and sell the organization on the prospect of being around for a long time.

The ethnographer as clinician. A few years ago Steve Barley did an ethnographic study of several radiology departments that were introducing computerized tomography equipment (CT scanners) (Barley, 1984a, 1984b). He obtained permission to become a member of these departments and to observe over a period of many months the day-to-day workings of the department. He gradually worked out a viable role for himself that involved minimum disruption of the work without excluding him from the observational scene.

Barley reported that as he became better known and trusted by the various radiological technicians, he found himself more and more drawn into day-to-day work issues that required his actively "helping." Initially this help was routine and he was told exactly what to do, such as holding a piece of equipment, reading a dial, or helping to move a patient. But as the fieldwork progressed, he was increasingly being asked to give advice on both technical and political matters. How should a technician proceed if the computer went down, how should a certain doctor be handled, what do you do with an uncooperative patient, how can we get some critical supplies that we have run out of, and so on?

The dilemma that Barley reports is that he knew perfectly well when he was stepping out of the ethnographic observer role and taking an active interventionist role, but he did not always know by what criteria he should make the judgment as to when to do this and how far to go in becoming de facto a working member of the group. Being an outsider with special knowledge and skills heightened this dilemma in that clinical expertise could be attributed to him beyond what he felt he possessed, and the refusal to help could compromise the future cooperativeness of the people being observed.

The manner in which he resolved the dilemma highlights that in the ethnographic relationship it is the researcher who has the initiative. Barley's primary focus was the changing nature of the technician's role so his credibility with the technicians had to remain high. He was less concerned about how the doctors in the units perceived him. Consequently he found himself helping the technicians actively while increasingly distancing himself from the doctors.

It may also be true that until the ethnographer becomes "helpful" he or she will not be truly accepted into the group and given access to the data he needs. Gideon Kunda (personal communication, 1986) reports working with an engineering group in a company that he wanted to study ethnographically and finding it very hard to be accepted because there was no natural role or niche for him. The climate changed dramatically when he participated in a company soccer game and helped the engineering group win. He was then given access to other meetings and generally treated as more of a "member." But it was his choice whether or not to participate.

Summary. As the above examples show, in practice the clinical and ethnographic roles can become highly intertwined, but this in no way implies that the roles are conceptually similar. In the Action and Multi Companies the contact was initiated *by them* because they wanted some help from me, whereas Barley and Kunda were in the radiology and engineering departments because they wanted access to gather data for their own theses. This difference in whose agenda is the source of the contact has major consequences for how the relationship unfolds and must be managed.

The implication of this situational reality is that the person who works with living human systems must be able to function in both the clinical and ethnographic role, and, furthermore, must be highly aware of when he or she is in which role so that neither relationship is fundamentally compromised.

**What Implicit Model
of the Organization Operates?**

The clinician typically starts with an "action research" model (Argyris, Putnam, & Smith, 1985; Lewin, 1948; Lippitt, Watson, & Westley, 1958; Schein, 1980), by which I mean that one begins with the assumption that *one cannot understand a human system without trying to change it.* The essential dynamics of the system are assumed to remain invisible to the passive observer. Only by becoming a member of the system and learning over a long period of time how it operates could the passive observer decipher it.

The clinician who is asked to help must have a model of how to improve the situation and is constrained by a timetable. Clinicians must therefore "intervene" with diagnostic or provocative questions, with interpretations, suggestions, or recommendations in order to *elicit* a response from the client. *The nature of that response then becomes primary diagnostic data for determining what may really be going on* (Schein, 1987).

The underlying model of the organization held by the clinician presumes, in fact, that *intervention precedes or is simultaneous with diagnosis,* and that improved diagnosis results from early efforts to intervene (Schein, 1969, 1987). Consulting models that advocate a period of diagnosis preceding intervention are, in my view, simply ignoring the obvious reality that their initial diagnostic efforts are themselves interventions of unknown consequence.

In my own experience, it is the observed anomalies, blank looks in response to simple questions, defensive denials and counterarguments, and various other kinds of emotional responses that occur in reaction to my own behavior that are the most valuable sources of insight into what is going on. The clinician should not be deliberately provocative because the primary goal is to establish a helping relationship, but when my well-intentioned behavior produces unexpected responses, instead of viewing my own behavior as a "mistake," it is important to recognize that the response to my behavior provides prime information that I need in order to become more helpful (Schein, 1987).

In other words, if one starts with an action research model, the primary source of organizational data is not what is "out there" to be observed, but is in the careful analysis of how members of the organization relate to the outsider, the clinician. This is the counterpart of what psychoanalysts would identify as the analysis of the "transference relationship" in that how the patient relates to the therapist directly may prove more valuable as a source of information than what the patient reports about various other situations (Kets de Vries & Miller, 1984).

The ethnographer's model of the organization is quite different in that it is built more on the assumption that the organization exists outside of the ethnographer's consciousness and is there to be understood and deciphered, not to be perturbed. The ethnographer may have to interact with members and may even have to provoke them at times in order to get diagnostic data, but the goal is to reveal the underlying structure that is out there, and the assumption dominates that if the ethnographer had sufficient time to observe passively it would eventually reveal itself.

Ethnographers of course differ on the degree to which they accept the assumption I am ascribing to them, with many arguing, just as the clinician would, that you must decipher the interactions that occur between subjects and investigators. If they are working from an interpretive model, they might even acknowledge that the reality they eventually report on is their own interpretation of those interactions, but even then I believe the assumption is lurking in the background that there is a reality out there to be deciphered and, more important, to be left reasonably intact.

Let me sharpen this point. Both ethnographers and clinicians will perturb the organization through provocative questions and the like, but they observe and interpret the responses differently. The clinician watches carefully how the client deals with what the clinician has done and uses that observation as "on line" data as evidence of how the organization works. Ethnographers watch how the subjects deal in general with the intervention, assuming themselves to be simply a general category of disturbance or intervention, and attempt to generalize from such responses how the system works. Clinicians assume that they have changed the system through their interventions, and, through changing it, have been able to watch it in action. Ethnographers assume they have lifted a curtain and had a chance to look behind it, but have not really changed anything.

Clinicians assume that they are supposed to change the system, and the opportunities to change it provide critical diagnostic data. Ethnographers assume that they are *not* supposed to change the system, but they must perturb it a bit at times in order to elicit a response to be observed or interpreted.

The models in action. In my efforts to understand the culture of the Multi Co. I stumbled upon a key assumption through observing what was happening to various communications that I sent to my contact client (Schein, 1985). I was trying to help them to become more innovative by circulating to all of the divisions and units new ideas that I found in some divisions and units of the company. I asked my contact to distribute memos outlining such innovations to all of the units, but found on at least three occasions during subsequent visits that the memos had never been circulated.

My first reaction was anger, but then I began to reflect on why such an obvious request had not been honored. I began to share my feelings with various informants and discovered first that some of them had had similar experiences. This led to some joint inquiry on our part and the eventual formulation that in the Multi Co. a person's job was such private turf that one never "invaded" it uninvited because that would risk making the person lose face. The implication would be that the person was not on top of his or her job and was not familiar with everything pertaining to it.

Once I had this insight, the two models outlined prescribe somewhat different next steps. In my role as ethnographer, I could now document how one part of this organizational culture functioned and spell out its ramifications by looking for further evidence of how it worked. In my role as clinician, given the goal to improve innovativeness, I had learned that the culture prevents unsolicited lateral communication and, therefore, if I wanted information to get to everyone I had to use other kinds of channels. By lodging my memos at more senior levels so that they would be passed down I could determine whether the assumptions about job turf also applied to vertical channels, and by sending my memos directly to all departments and divisions I could test readiness to accept ideas if they came from a paid outside expert. Since I was being paid to help, I intervened by sending memos directly to persons in more senior roles and watched carefully how the information was then passed or not passed. This intervention worked well enough (in the sense that information began to circulate) that I did not try sending things directly.

Summary. The clinician starts with an action research model of the organization built on the assumption that the only way to understand an organization is to change it, and that the only way to understanding, therefore, lies through deliberate intervention and the deciphering of the responses to the intervention. The ethnographer starts with the assumption that the organization is there to be understood and left intact, so interventions would be used only as practical necessities and would be designed to make as little change in the organization as possible.

Whose Needs Drive the Process of Inquiry and Data Gathering?

In the clinical model, the source and focus of energy is in the client system. Somebody wants some help, sees a problem, wants to cope better with some task, wants an answer to some question, wants relief from some undesirable condition. The client not only initiates this process but continues to fuel it through the continuation of the request for help, and the process terminates when the client no longer has the energy or resources to continue, or the relationship becomes psychologically untenable. This initiative and continued commitment is symbolized and made operational by the client's willingness to pay for the services rendered.

In contrast, the ethnographer initiates the process of inquiry by seeking out the relevant organization and uses his or her own energy to gain entry, form a relationship, and elicit interest and motivation from the client on a problem that is at the outset the focus of the ethnographer. Occasionally organizations will volunteer to be studied and seek out a historian or ethnographer to focus on something they want documented or analyzed, but this is the exception and often involves a complex negotiation around who will own the data and what will be published. This very complexity signals that the more natural relationship is the one where the ethnographer specifies what his or her own needs are and elicits agreement from the organization.

Clinicians are, of course, not passive in that they can accept or reject any given request for help, and can, through their own interventions, guide the focus of inquiry into areas that may fall closer to their own interests. But professional responsibility dictates that they must help the client in the areas that the client has specified; they do not have an open hunting license to work on any problem that they may encounter or that may interest them.

Ethnographers, though initially strongly focused on their own research needs, will often have those interests modified by what they encounter as they begin to study the organization. As they get pushed into clinical situations, as they uncover phenomena that they may not have been aware of, they become more responsive to the interests and problems of the system they are studying, but their professional responsibility remains to their academic goals and they will put limits on how much the subject's interests will be allowed to divert them from those goals.

The fact that the ethnographer is not getting paid by the client is essential in providing him or her the intellectual and emotional freedom to pursue those academic interests. Once pay is involved, some clinical obligation has been undertaken to provide some form of help, and that automatically shifts the source of focus and energy to the client.

The Psychological Contract
in the Two Situations

The various points made above can best be focused and sharpened by examining what the *psychological contract* is between clinician and clients on the one hand, and ethnographer and subjects on the other hand. By psychological contract I mean the unspoken expectations that operate between the parties and that define what behavior is considered normal or abnormal, what behavior is defined as good or bad, and what defines success or failure in the relationship (Schein, 1980). The psychological contract usually has components that operate from the very outset between the parties, based on their prior experience and their stereotypes of what certain relationships imply, but as the relationship unfolds, the contract gets renegotiated in complex ways.

At the most basic level, in the clinical relationship the client expects to pay fees and expenses in exchange for which he or she will experience some improvement or obtain some help in a defined problem area. The clinician expects to get fees, expenses, and the motivation and cooperation of the client in working on the problem, in exchange for which he or she will use process, diagnostic, and intervention skills to provide whatever help is possible in the situation. Both parties will accept some constraints based on the definition of the problem, the amount of time allocated to the problem, the defined area of expertise of the clinician, the size of the fees, and the budget of the client.

The psychological contract in the case of the ethnographer entering an organization is quite different. The "subject" expects to give the ethnographer access to various organizational settings, make introductions, and in other ways smooth the way in exchange for which he or she will ultimately obtain some feedback on what the research results revealed, which, in turn, will provide insights that would permit the organization to be more effective. The subject makes the implicit assumption (sometimes stated explicitly as a condition for cooperation) that the ethnographer will know how to behave in such a way as not to be too obtrusive, not to disturb members of the organization too much, not to ask embarrassing questions, and, by and large, pay his or her own expenses.

Ethnographers implicitly agree because their model of the organization requires that they not be too obtrusive lest they change the very thing they are trying to study. They expect to be given access and help in entering the organization in exchange for which they will provide whatever feedback they consider appropriate to help the subject learn something useful about his or her organization. Both parties have to agree on what the ethnographer will be permitted to make public in professional journals or other publications, whether or not the organization or its members will be explicitly identified, how long the project will take, and how feedback will be provided.

Expectations about termination in the clinical relationship generally focus on the client. The project is over when the client feels that enough help has been provided. If the clinician does not agree, he or she can attempt to convince the client to continue, but the ultimate vote is in the client's hands because he or she is paying the bills. On the other hand, the clinician can, in some instances, terminate the project early if he or she feels that no help is possible or that nothing further can be done. If the client wishes to continue, professional norms dictate that the clinician must explain clearly why he or she feels continuing would not be fruitful even if the client is willing to continue to pay the fees.

In the ethnographic situation, the project is finished when the ethnographer has decided that he or she has enough data to meet his or her own research goals, when the organization was understood to his or her own level of satisfaction. If, in the meantime, the ethnographer has alienated the members of the system he or she may be thrown out earlier than his or her own plans would call for, but the basic decision on when things are finished is the ethnographer's.

Interestingly, the ethnographer's job is not finished when the fieldwork is finished. The problem of analyzing the data, deciding what has been learned, and how to present it are integral to the ethnographic task and may require a great deal of time and effort after the relationship with the field site has been severed (Van Maanen, 1987). In contrast, the integral part of the clinician's work is done when the client defines the point of termination. If the clinician then spends years mulling over what he or she has learned from the case, this is not typically thought of as part of the clinical work.

Understanding versus help. In the clinical model, understanding fully what is going on is subordinated to fixing whatever problem the client wanted fixed. There is nothing in the psychological contract that obligates the clinician to understand what is going on provided he or she has been helpful in facilitating getting the problem fixed.

In the ethnographic model, understanding is the primary goal, even if that understanding reveals some serious problems in the organization about which something should be done. The psychological contract for the ethnographer does not obligate him or her to do anything about the problem, sometimes not even to give feedback about it if it falls outside the agreed upon area of inquiry.

This situation leads to a further contrast. Clinicians may well be frustrated by the fact that they have been helpful without really having understood the dynamics of the situation fully enough. Part of them would like to redefine the relationship toward the ethnographic so that their need for learning and understanding could be fully met. On the other hand, ethnographers may well be frustrated by the fact that their inquiry has revealed some problems that require attention. Part of them would like to redefine the relationship toward the clinical so that they would be "licensed" to become more active in helping. Why then do the two roles not come together more easily? Why not even advocate that the two roles should be played simultaneously?

The answer may lie in another part of the psychological contract, in the implicit rules of what constitutes *unethical* behavior on the part of the inquirer. Clinicians are *legally* liable in the sense that they can be sued for malpractice, where malpractice is defined as incompetent delivery of promised help, the actual harming of the client, or the taking of fees for services not actually delivered. This point is obvious in states that have licensing laws for clinical psychologists and counselors. Organization development consultants have attempted to spell out codes of ethics that could become the basis of a legal definition of malpractice. Some years back the National Training Laboratories were sued by the relative of a person who had allegedly been injured by attendance at a sensitivity training session on the grounds that sensitivity training was "therapy" not education. Rare as these examples may be, they clearly show that the clinical, therapeutic perspective sets up a psychological contract in which clients feels vulnerable and, therefore, must defend themselves.

What legal liability do ethnographers have? They can be sued for libel or slander if they publish material in a scientifically irresponsible manner by not adequately disguising identities, revealing confidential information, or in other ways making the organization vulnerable by what has been publicly revealed about it. The ethnographers' implicit contract is to locate the truth and to reveal it only in a scientifically responsible manner.

Note that if clinicians try to become ethnographers and publish their results, they then incur the ethnographers' liability. Similarly, if ethnographers try to help with problems that may have been uncovered, they make themselves liable for malpractice. What this analysis suggests is that both roles can be played only *if the individual has competence in both areas*. Clinicians not trained in the rigorous methods of ethnography, and ethnographers without clinical training, should be careful about mixing those roles. More will be said about this when we examine the training for such roles.

Insider activist roles. Of course, either the clinician or the ethnographer can decide to switch to an internal activist role by intervening in a managerial or leadership capacity. In either role one can discover that a person or group has a problem that requires direct intervention on their behalf and choose to become their leader or champion. But when the outsider abandons his or her outsider role and becomes a direct interventionist inside the system, he or she accepts other risks and liabilities having to do with giving up his or her external power base.

Both the clinician and the ethnographer have important outside reference groups to draw on for guidance, support, and standards. If the person joins the organizational fray, so to speak, the person makes himself or herself part of the political power system of the organization and must take the consequences. For example, some years ago I was doing an interview survey of a group of engineers on behalf of the senior management of an industrial research laboratory. The many grievances that emerged in the interviews convinced me that the engineers needed some help in getting their message across so I not only biased the data I obtained from them to highlight their grievances, but in subsequent meetings with management found myself directly arguing for improvements on behalf of the engineers. I was acting more as an internal representative of the engineering group than as a clinician/consultant trying to improve the overall situation in the lab.

Not unexpectedly, management did not take kindly to my advocacy role, cut off the information feedback prematurely, and terminated the consulting relationship so that I lost access to the organization immediately. My taking an advocacy position made it difficult to draw on my outsider clinical role as a basis for preserving some kind of relationship so, in the end, I found that I would have been more helpful to the engineers had I managed to remain in the neutral intermediary role.

In this example I also violated some of the requirements of the ethnographic role in that I made assumptions about what was really going on without sufficient data on what was going on in other parts of the organization. I had not spent enough time with management to determine how they viewed the situation, what their complaints were about the engineers, and what had happened in the past between the two groups. Had I obtained such data I might have had a better understanding of how to intervene.

Misattributions by the client as sources of difficulty. One of the most difficult aspects of the psychological contract is that the client or subject may have silent expectations based on his attributing to the clinician or ethnographer motives, skills, and attitudes that they may not, in fact, have. Thus one can find oneself disappointing organizational insiders without even knowing that one is doing so. Both clinicians and ethnographers have to be sensitive to this pitfall and make expectations about roles as explicit as possible whenever appropriate opportunities arise.

For example, in the clinical model an important distinction in my own work is between *process* consultation that highlights helping the client to solve his or her own problems and *expert* consulting that puts the clinician into a doctor or expert role from which he or she prescribes solutions (Schein, 1969, 1987). I am often asked by organization members to give advice on how to organize or manage something that falls well outside my area of expertise, and then find myself having to "disappoint" the client by not providing a ready answer.

Or the client assumes that my role is to gather all of the organizational "dirty laundry" so I am regaled with horror stories about mismanagement on the theory that this information will now be passed to the right quarters and the malfunctioning parts of the organization will be fixed. When things are not fixed there is again disappointment.

Furthermore, the client may assume that as a clinician I am competent to evaluate people and willing to do so. I have often been asked in the middle of a project to make evaluative comments on various managers and employees I may have met, and then have to reexplain that I do not consider that as part of my role if it was not specifically mentioned and agreed to at the outset. If it is mentioned at the outset or if I sense that such expectations may arise I have to be explicit in saying that I will not evaluate individuals because it has been my experience that once such evaluations are done members of the organization cease to provide me with valid data for fear that it will reflect badly on them.

On the other hand, I have not found it helpful to try to anticipate all of these issues with elaborate attempts to make all aspects of the psychological contract explicit, because the client may get so put off by all of the statements about what the consultant will or will not do that it constrains the relationship unnecessarily. Only a few general points about confidentiality and my concept of how I will help seem to suffice, provided I am ready to discuss the psychological contract whenever issues arise as the project proceeds.

The ethnographer has similar problems, having to do with what subjects attribute to academic researchers. The ethnographer may be seen as having esoteric knowledge, x-ray vision, extraordinary insights into organizational dynamics, and knowledge of how things should work. While he or she is trying to learn how things do work in the organization, members of the organization may be busily trying to learn from him or her things that may be of use to them. If one fails to respond to such needs on the part of the subjects, the risk becomes one of alienating them and being seen only as a nuisance.

What seems often to work best in these situations is to expand the relationship around informal events such as being helpful on routine work tasks, during mealtimes, as a member of the company sports team, and the like. The goal for the ethnographer is to demystify himself or herself to become one of the gang. The clinician, on the other hand, does *not* want to become one of the gang because a clinician's effectiveness depends more on the assumed role of outsider neutrality.

Summary and Conclusions

I have tried to highlight the difference between the role of the organizational clinician and the ethnographer by addressing several critical questions: (1) Who initiates and drives the process? (2) What is the implicit model of the organization held by each? (3) Whose needs drive the process of inquiry? (4) What is the psychological contract operating between outsider and insider?

As one examines the contrasts between the two roles in terms of each of these questions it becomes clear that they are based on quite different premises and assumptions about the goal of the inquiry process (help versus understanding), about the nature of organizational research (action research versus participation, observation, and interpretation), and what is fundamentally exchanged between the outsider and insider (help for pay versus access for feedback).

I noted that in the field there are strong pressures for the roles to merge but that if the outsider is not careful in analyzing what role should be assumed and manages the process accordingly, the outsider runs into some pitfalls and assumes some risks that can have severe consequences (legal liability for malpractice versus libel or slander).

In this chapter I have attempted to clarify the fundamental difference in the models, roles, and perspectives. In the next chapter I want to elaborate some of the consequences of these differences for the process of acquiring, analyzing, and validating data about human systems.

3. GATHERING, ANALYZING, AND VALIDATING DATA

Conceptual Focus and
Type of Data Gathered

The clinical and ethnographic perspectives lead to different foci of inquiry and to different methods of data gathering. The clinical perspective is, by definition, oriented toward concepts of health and pathology, toward problem areas that require remedial action, toward the dynamics of change and "improvement." It is therefore *normative* in its orientation and requires underlying theories that provide normative direction—concepts of health, effectiveness, growth, innovation, integration, and the like.

These underlying theories or models of "system health" (Bennis, 1962) may or may not remain implicit, but they are always there, by definition. The clinical perspective therefore is theory linked whether the clinician is consciously aware of this fact or not. This point is crucially important because much of the controversy around the clinical method has to do less with the tactics of intervention and more with the underlying theories on which such interventions are based. One organizational consultant may be operating from psychoanalytic theory (Kets de Vries & Miller, 1984; Levinson, 1972), while another starts with sociotechnical theory (Rice, 1963; Trist, Higgin, Murray, & Pollack, 1963), yet they may make very similar interventions in the short run. How their colleagues react to their later written analyses will have more to do with their reaction to the theories than to the interventions.

The underlying theory of organizational health is not the only filter that the clinician operates with. The clinician is also focused, by definition, on the client's initial problem statement, the reasons given for why the clinician was invited into the organization in the first place. Although the clinician may attempt to be totally open and neutral with respect to the kind of data that will be listened for and observed, the clinician will always be screening and filtering those data in terms of the client's initial formulation of the problem, and will use data diagnostically to get a better sense of what may be going on with respect to the client and his organization.

In the clinician's experiential background will be other cases of organizational pathology and how they were dealt with in order to use them as a basis for comparison and as a source of diagnostic ideas and insights. This background will operate as a filter as well in that some categories of initial problem statements by the client will be perceived by the clinician as outside his or her range of expertise, and result in an initial refusal to get involved. Or certain categories of problem formulation will clearly interest the clinician more and will motivate the clinician to "sell" his or her services more in those areas by showing interest, claiming experience and skill, and so on.

In contrast, the ethnographic perspective requires investigators to open themselves as much as possible to whatever they will find in the setting to be investigated. The investigator will start with research goals, and will inevitably have his or her own preferred concepts and categories for analyzing data, but these will be referenced more to his or her own research agenda than to either theories of system health or formulations of problems that may be reported by subjects in the organization.

The ethnographer's categories of analysis are therefore likely to be broader, to deal much more with the total context of the situation he or she is studying, and to be related to sociological, anthropological, and social psychological theory. Such theories are, of course, of value to the clinicians as well, but they are not as relevant to the immediate fulfillment of their psychological contract. More essential to the clinician would be psychological theories, interpersonal theory, group theory, and those portions of systems theory that deal particularly with systems health and the process of improving system effectiveness.

In summary, both clinicians and ethnographers start their inquiry processes with a degree of conceptual bias and, at the same time, with a conscious effort to open themselves up as much as possible to the data at hand, but the nature of the biases are quite different in the two cases leading them to listen for and observe different things, referenced in the case of the clinician to the *client's* stated problem and, in the case of ethnographers, to *their own research goals.*

Depth and level of detail. The clinician's role requires an analysis "in-depth" in that the area of agreed upon pathology must be pursued until enough insight has been produced to discover a remedial intervention. This means that the inquiry may be very limited in terms of "breadth" in that the clinician is licensed to go into only those areas that appear to be relevant to the problem the clinician and the client are working on. On the other hand, the clinician has the license to ask embarrassing questions, to elicit confidential information, and to ask for the airing of organizational "dirty laundry," provided there is some connection to the problem being worked on. They are licensed to encourage their client informants to "confess," to tell what is "really going on" as they see it and, in this sense to gain a "deeper" dynamic understanding of what is happening and why it is happening.

Such probing often leads to insights about what "really happened" and how things "really work" around limited areas of organizational functioning because people in the organization are motivated by their need to solve problems to tell what is really going on from their point of view. This is not to say that there will be an automatic dropping of the kinds of psychological defenses and face-protecting maneuvers that one would see in individual counseling, but that there is a license granted to the clinician to work on those defenses and to help the client to go beyond them in the interest of organization improvement. The clinical relationship also encourages an exploration of motives and intentions by providing some picture of the dynamic forces that may be acting in the situation. As we will see below, when motives and intentions are revealed by some of the more powerful people in the organization to whom the clinician has access, it suddenly clarifies many of the consequent events that may be observed by those who are studying by ethnographic means what is happening in other parts of the organization.

The ethnographer is generally more concerned with completeness of description so that the total situation can be understood by the reader. If possible, ethnographers strive for "thick description" (Geertz, 1973; Van Maanen, 1987), which is an effort to provide enough concrete detail to bring a given situation vividly to life so that the reader can empathize with it. So while the clinician may learn a great deal about a particular process in the organization, he or she may learn relatively little about the context and related goings on; the ethnographer will learn a great deal about the context, related matters, and how things work generally at a considerable level of detail, but may miss how a particular process works in depth unless that particular process becomes a focus of inquiry. In those cases where ethnographers are trying to decipher something in depth they probably find themselves using elements of the clinical perspective by trying to elicit more confidential information from informants who have something to gain by revealing it. But their ability to do this will depend on how their psychological contract with the subject is perceived.

Who learns "more"? Inevitably the question arises as to who learns more about the reality or truth of what may be going on. This analysis suggests that the question itself is too simplistic. The two perspectives lead to different levels of knowledge, but the clinical knowledge is often underutilized and undercredited because it is not gathered by traditional models of scientific inquiry. Yet the clinician often has access to data that the ethnographer will never get because the client is not motivated to reveal it, and the clinician often has access to levels of the organization that the ethnographer finds difficult to penetrate. The point I want to emphasize is that the nature of the data that will be deliberately and consciously revealed by members of the organization is a function of the psychological contract that is operating, and it is only in the clinical situation where the informant is truly motivated to reveal what he believes to be "really going on" because he is paying the outsider to provide help.

The ethnographer will, or course, often take the theoretical position that what clients believe to be really going on is not in fact what a carefully documented study would show to be the dynamic as observed by an outsider, so a question arises of who "really" learns what is "really going on," or how do we determine what is "valid data" in organizational inquiry?

If the ethnographer believes in the validity of data revealed in confidence by organizational members, the ethnographer can, of course, approximate the clinical situation in terms of the *depth* of the data elicited. But there may still be an important difference in terms of who the ethnographer has access to as contrasted with who the clinician has access to. The ethnographer often looks for informants who have motives to "reveal" things—whistle blowers, alienated employees, revolutionaries of various sorts, people who want to show off what they know—but it should be recognized that such people are more likely to be found in the *lower* levels of organizations so that this source of data has an intrinsic organizational bias toward members with less formal power, and hence an antiestablishment bias.

On the other hand, the clinicians in their role as consultants are often brought in near the top of organizations so that their data bias is to learn more quickly how people at the power center view things, and, by virtue of learning more about how they really view the world, may be more likely to develop a proestablishment bias.

But the biases are not symmetrical. Because organizations are power-based hierarchies, access to how powerful people view things and make their decisions often reveals the causes of organizational events throughout the organization more quickly and in greater depth than access at lower levels. I am not arguing that knowledge of what higher levels are doing automatically makes it possible to infer what is going on at lower levels. Indeed, we often err by assuming that the intentions of higher levels are a good indicator of outcomes at lower levels, something that ethnographers have often shown to be fallacious. But the *deciphering* problem is asymmetrical. *It is easier for the clinician with access at the top to learn what the impact of high-level decisions is at the lower levels than it is for ethnographers who see life in the middle or at the bottom of an organization to infer and decipher what decisions may have been made at the top that led to what they observe.* There is no incentive for the top people to reveal their thinking unless they are in a clinical relationship where they are seeking help.

Another way of putting this is in terms of Goffman's concept of front- and backstage (Goffman, 1959). The clinician is often taken "backstage" immediately because clients are attempting to work backstage issues and problems in relation to their feelings of not being able to get certain things accomplished. But, in fact, what the clinician initially sees is the *client's own view* of what is happening in *one* part of the backstage. Unless the clinician can become something of a participant observer and take an ethnographic view, he or she may never be exposed to the "fronts" that are involved. The managers who tell me what their problems are may never be directly observed by me.

On the other hand, the ethnographer sees the action on the stage, the various fronts, but unless special relationships with the actors are developed, the ethnographer may never find out why certain things happened the way they did, and he or she may never have access to why people at higher levels did the things they did, even though the consequences of their action are highly visible. And the asymmetry of the situation derives from my hypothesis that it is easier for the clinician to move into the front stage areas than for the ethnographer to move into the backstage areas.

Given this asymmetry in what is potentially available as data, one is tempted to argue that we will never fully understand organizations until clinicians and ethnographers begin to work together to pool their insights or until a generation of clinician/scholars is trained in both sets of roles and skills.

Some illustrative examples. In the previously referred to Action Co. it has been observed over and over again by members and by ethnographers that the organization elicits very high levels of motivation from its engineers and technicians; it may be one of the few companies in the world where the dual ladder of rewarding both technical and managerial personnel actually works. One observes people in high-level technical positions, one sees managers moving from managerial to technical jobs, and when one inquires, one finds that people value technical positions. There is not the pressure to go into management that one so often finds in other organizations as "the only way to get ahead." From an observed and ethnographic point of view one could describe this organization as having successfully managed to introduce the "dual ladder," and one can describe in detail how it works for the individual engineer.

In my role as consultant to the executive committee of this company, I was able not only to observe how senior management viewed these matters, but, more important, I heard the president and founder of the company passionately speak out in favor of technical careers. He felt that the company could succeed only if it could make its engineers feel that they had a lifetime career in the organization as engineers, and that they would never have to go into management if they did not really feel like it or were not exceptionally good at it. He felt very deeply about this and it became apparent that this passion carried over into strong messages to the organization. He insisted on giving higher-ranking jobs to engineers, he consulted them frequently on important organizational matters, he protected them from the financial and other controls that might have undermined their work, and he publicly criticized management while glorifying engineering.

Is this additional knowledge gained in the clinical context important to understanding what is going on, given that it is consistent with the observations already made at lower levels? In fact it turns out to be crucial because I witnessed repeatedly how the traditional models of hierarchical organization, with their emphasis on management, were touted by lower levels of management as the way to develop the organization. The "normal" dynamic in the organization was to favor the managerial roles, and it was only because of the excessive emphasis that the president and founder put on the technical ladder that it survived at all. If the ethnographer did not know of all the incidents that occurred at the top of the organization that protected engineering from strong marketing, sales, manufacturing, and financial managers, he would have no way of explaining why the dual-ladder system was working.

This "extra" knowledge, based on clinical data, is crucial for developing broader insight into organizations because it is typically reported that dual ladders do not work as well as they are supposed to. My hypothesis based on this case would be that the inherent bias in organizations toward management being the elite and critical function is so strong that only a passionately motivated chief executive or founder has enough leverage to compensate for such forces and to produce a balanced dual ladder that will work.

In another organization it was observed ethnographically that the human resource function was having a difficult time developing and imposing consistent standards for evaluating and rewarding employee performance across the several divisions of the organization. The members of the corporate personnel department were in constant conflict with the personnel representatives from the divisions over who should have the ultimate power to determine basic policy of how much to pay, how much stock to give to different categories of employees, and how to assess performance.

The company had an explicit written human resource policy of which it was very proud, and it also had a business philosophy of decentralization. That is, each division was allowed to manage its own business affairs. The conflict arose over whether human resource policy fell under the corporate umbrella or was the business of the divisions.

I was brought into the organization by the president to help in the formation of a top management team and, to this end, was invited to sit in on some meetings of the new group. As it happened, the agenda of one of these meetings was to be a discussion of the hiring of a new vice president for Human Resources. As I listened to the discussion it became suddenly very clear why there was conflict down the line.

The primary function of the new vice president was to become a strong mediator between the president who represented the corporate position of developing a coherent human resource policy and two very strong division managers who really wanted the freedom to operate in their own way. I observed that when one of these division managers took a strong stand to allow one of his people to be treated differently from what the policy called for, the president allowed the exception. I also observed that when the then director of Human Resources came in with some proposals for the development of a common human resource inventory, one division manager got impatient with the whole idea, said it was a waste of time, and *was not overruled by the president*. This behavior sent a clear message to the director of Human Resources as to where the power really lay and put him into the position of having to try to implement policies that the president was not prepared to back personally over the objections of his division managers.

In talking to the president, I learned that he wanted ultimately to have a more coherent policy and believed in it very strongly, but he also recognized that without strong division management the company would not succeed, so he had to allow his division managers levels of autonomy that would, in the short run, create inconsistencies in policy. He wanted them to learn and to develop so that eventually a more common policy would emerge.

In order to decipher what was going on in this organization at all levels one has to know that the president is ambivalent about his own human resource policy, that he will compromise it if strong division managers subvert it, and will allow time while the division managers learn and develop. He will work the issue out by seeking a strong vice president for Human Resources who can effectively mediate between himself and the division heads. All of this I believe is crucial knowledge if one is to help this organization and if one is to understand what is happening "down in the trenches."

Another example will illustrate the potential of combined knowledge where it is not initially available. In his *Tales of the Field*, Van Maanen (1987) describes the difficulty of getting access to a police department as a site for ethnographic work. He reported that he had been turned down by over fifteen departments and finally found one through the "lucky" contact of finding a professor in his graduate school who had done some sensitivity training for the management of the police department in "Union City." This professor who had established a clinical relationship with the Union City management was then instrumental in getting Van Maanen the contacts needed to get into and study the organization.

What I find especially intriguing in this example is that Van Maanen cites it as a case of how entry was managed, but does not discuss the potential implications of working in a department in which senior management had had some sensitivity training. What could be inferred about this organization from this bit of data, and would it have altered some of Van Maanen's understanding of what he later learned in his role as ethnographer if he had analyzed some of his data together with the professor who had done the sensitivity training and presumably knew something, therefore, about the motives, attitudes, and intentions of the top people in the department?

In summary, what the clinician often sees in working with the power centers is the motives and intentions of key people, but not the consequences of what they do. In contrast, the ethnographer often sees the consequences very clearly but cannot decipher their origins because he may not be able to get at the motives and intentions of the top people. Only when both perspectives and knowledge bases are brought to bear on the situation does it become clearly understandable.

Data biases based on the psychological contract. In both the clinical and ethnographic relationship there will be presentational biases to be analyzed that derive from the different psychological contracts in the relationships. The client wants to present a proper picture to the clinician—he must reveal some kind of presentational problem to justify calling in the helper, but he will not necessarily reveal the real problem early in the relationship and he will calibrate carefully the degree to which the clinician provides the "psychological safety" that would permit him to tell what he is really feeling and seeing.

One of the arguments I have made for a process consultation model over the traditional model of the consultant as an expert or doctor is that the process model makes it easier for clients to let their hair down and reveal what is really bothering them because the process model, by assuming that clients will be able to help themselves, empowers clients and helps them to overcome the psychological trauma of having to admit a problem in the first place. In any case, the kinds of presentational issues, defense mechanisms, and biases that clients exhibit have been fairly well documented, and much of the training of the clinician concerns how to deal with them. As was mentioned in the previous chapter, one of the major sources of clinical insight is, in fact, the biases that the client reveals in the early interactions with the clinician (Schein, 1987).

The situation for ethnographers is more complex, because their role in the organization is often initially more ambiguous. It is easier to project onto ethnographers all kinds of images, and, if those projections remain implicit, it will be harder for ethnographers to decipher how they are being handled by the members of the organization. Unless they enter the organization completely unobtrusively by literally becoming a participant, they will be subject to various fantasies about their role, and those fantasies will bias how members present themselves to ethnographers (Van Maanen, 1987). Much of the technology of gathering ethnographic data deals with this dilemma so I will not discuss it further here, except to underscore that it is a dilemma that must be faced.

In this area as well, it would probably be helpful to organizational studies if clinicians could observe the evolution of an ethnographic study and if ethnographers could observe the meetings between a clinician and his clients. The problem, of course, is that either of these desirable alternatives creates new organizational scenes that may be unacceptable to members of the organization, or may elicit still more biased behavior based on the fantasies that members have about what may be going on.

The next best thing is to have the clinician and ethnographer, who have both been exposed to the same organization, share their notes and insights to see whether a combined view illuminates organizational phenomena further. A further example will attempt to illustrate these issues.

Multiple data sources in the Allen Financial Services Co. One of my ongoing consulting projects was initiated by a division manager, Mr. Ralston, who wanted help in thinking through various programs of sociotechnical change he had initiated in his division. He wanted to redesign the basic work of the unit, thereby eliminating one managerial level and thus reducing costs, at the same time he wanted to enlarge the jobs of the basic operators in the organization by having them have more contact with customers. In addition, he wanted the whole unit to become more marketing oriented, he wanted to increase productivity and have a zero-defects quality program, and he had initiated various other programs to increase participation and communication across levels.

Ralston also wanted his immediate subordinates, the department heads, to become more of a collaborative team that would support the various other efforts. The basic vision was to create a situation where an operations group that had traditionally been measured only in terms of its costs could, by using more advanced information technology and taking more of a marketing orientation, build business and make profits for the Allen Co.

In my clinical role I worked with Ralston on his own perceptions of what was and was not working, his own sense of overload, some of his frustration that things were not moving along as rapidly as they should be, and his problems of how best to implement all of his programs. Ralston also thought it would be a good idea if I met his subordinates and worked my way down in the organization to get a feel for what was going on and how best to help.

As I began to meet other people spontaneously during my visits, and as Ralston asked me to meet with others to get their input (e.g., his immediate subordinates and various staff people), I became exposed to other data that suggested a real communication gap between Ralston and some of his people. People felt overloaded and unable to implement all of the things Ralston wanted and they felt unable to get the message across to him that this overload condition existed. So they set their own priorities and responded primarily to those things that Ralston measured explicitly and regularly.

From an ethnographic perspective, these data could have been analyzed as an interesting case of organizational dynamics and the problems of implementing technological changes without full understanding of their sociotechnical consequences. From a clinical perspective, the problem was how to open up channels of communication so that Ralston's goals could be met without creating problems for his subordinates that they could not handle. I became, in part, a communication channel to "convince" Ralston that he had to set priorities so that his organization could focus its efforts on those things that were most consequential, and to "convince" the department heads that they could communicate with Ralston and achieve many of his goals if they became more of a team and helped each other.

I learned a tremendous amount as I talked to more and more people in the organization about the dynamics of change and the problems of implementing new ideas. I learned how the vision of a senior manager gradually gets altered and eroded as it works its way through the layers of the organization, and this knowledge was, in fact, essential for helping Ralston and his organization to cope with its collective goals. As a clinician I became a kind of intermediary working on behalf of the whole organization, but I needed detailed information about what was going on lower in the organization in order to make constructive interventions.

My awareness of the asymmetry of knowledge as a function of the level at which one is working came about through the coincidence that Ralston had also asked another person to interview people all through the division to "document" the change program from a much more neutral ethnographic view. In my meetings with this person we found that we had very different data sets because she had done more work at the lower levels and was working her way up, while I was starting at the top and working my way down. As we discussed what was going on in the division we found that important insights could be obtained from comparing our views, but that the data from the top were essential to the understanding of the total situation.

For example, my knowledge that Ralston was deeply committed to his vision of the future organization and would do everything in his power to make it happen certainly influenced my approach to working with his subordinates in the sense that if they dug in their heels I knew that they were, in a sense, fighting a battle that they would eventually lose. In my go-between consultant role I had to ensure that they understood clearly how committed Ralston was to his goals.

Summary. I have tried to show that the clinical and ethnographic perspective lead to focusing on different kinds of data, based at the outset on the different conceptual models that the inquirer brings into the situation. The clinician starts with normative models and becomes descriptive in his or her efforts to decipher what is going on. The ethnographer starts with descriptive models and may or may not become normative depending upon the scientific problem he or she has selected.

The data are further influenced by the expectations and attributions of the clients and subjects. The clinician will obtain deeper data about more limited areas, while the ethnographer will obtain more superficial data about broader areas. The clinician will be shown dirty laundry and told secrets by people high up in the organization if they are the clients, while the ethnographer is more likely to see such data from the organization's middle or lower levels. The clinician will learn a lot about motives and intentions in the power centers, while the ethnographer will learn a lot about how things actually work out, the consequences of behavior taken by people in power.

Both sets of data are probably necessary in order to understand any human system, hence ways must be found for a person to take both perspectives or for clinicians and ethnographers to learn to work with each other on the same projects if real understanding of organizational realities is to be attained.

Determination of Scientific Validity

How do clinicians and ethnographers differ, if they do, in how they validate what they have found out? The ethnographer ultimately uses the traditional scientific criterion of *replicability*. If another ethnographer goes into the same human system, will he or she observe the same kinds of things? The ethnographer also relies on *internal consistency* and on giving enough detail of what is going on to give *credibility* to the argument (Van Maanen, 1987). The strong test of this is to give the data back to the group studied and ask them if they have been accurately depicted, but this turns out to be problematical because of unknown biases in the group's tendency to accept or deny data about itself.

Another strong test is the "member test"—can the ethnographer pass as a member of the group he or she is studying? As ethnographers have increasingly abandoned their own assumption that pure observation is possible, that they can simply be a camera, and have acknowledged how much of what they see and report to be an interpretive process, the problems of reliability and validity have grown apace.

Hence ultimately only replicability will truly validate ethnographic data in that the assumption still operates that there is "something" out there to be observed and interpreted and not to be disturbed too much, even though historically replicability has itself been difficult to achieve consistently. But there is little doubt that a student of a culture can tell a person who is about to visit that culture a great deal about what he will see there, and indeed the predicted things will be seen.

For clinicians, the situation is more complicated because one of the assumptions clinicians make is that their very presence changes the situation and, in fact, changing it is one of the reasons for being present. The clinical process will always change situations to an unknown degree that makes replication a difficult criterion unless one finds many cases that display essentially similar characteristics at the outset and studies them comparatively. In the case of organizational research this is less likely to work than in the case of individual research because each organization has so many contextually and historically unique features.

Clinicians do recognize common features in organizational situations based upon their own experience and discussion with others, and thus may start with hunches as to what may be going on, but they cannot test those hunches until they have made some sort of intervention. For clinicians, the ultimate validation test, then, is whether or not they can *predict the results of a given intervention.* If they can, such predicted responses validate their model or theory of what is happening. The validation is in the dynamic process itself, and depends not on replication so much as successful prediction. Replication again comes in at the dynamic process level, however, in that clinicians can predict that "every time I do this, the following thing will happen," or can tell their client "every time you do that, the following thing will happen."

For example, in the Allen Co. cited above, once I knew how the managers under Ralston felt, I could safely predict that every time he launched a new program, some other program of his would be put on the shelf, and that the level of tension and resistance in the organization would increase. On the other hand, I could also predict that if Ralston clearly stated his priorities and what he would really pay attention to, those programs would be carried forth effectively and tension in the organization would decrease.

I could also theorize about what was going on inside Ralston's head and predict how he would respond to various kinds of interventions. My degree of understanding of the situation could then be tested by making certain interventions and seeing whether or not Ralston responded predictably. For example, I hypothesized from listening to Ralston that he was very proud of what he and his group had already accomplished and that his frustration was akin to the frustration of a parent whose children are disappointing him even though he is basically very proud of them. If that was a tenable hypothesis he should respond positively to evidence that the department heads were in fact making every effort to support the program and that he would defend them if evidence were brought out that they were incompetent or recalcitrant.

The clinician's professional responsibility would preclude "experimenting" by making both types of interventions, so the prediction can be tested only on what the clinician regards as constructive or facilitative interventions. In the above case, then, only the first possibility could be tested, but it did get tested repeatedly and I got the distinct feeling that Ralston was always very pleased and relieved when one could show him any evidence of support on the part of the subordinates.

Improvement as validation. The clinician is always operating in a context in which problems are identified and goals for improvement are set. Correct prediction of how the client will respond to interventions can serve as an intermediate validating criterion, but actual improvement of the situation or the removal of problems would be the ultimate criterion.

The problem with using improvement as a criterion is that it does not necessarily reveal the causal links. As clinicians well know, improvement oten takes place without them knowing precisely why or even how it occurred. If improvement does *not* occur as predicted, the clinician clearly has disconfirmed his or her hypotheses, but if improvement does take place it does not necessarily support those hypotheses.

In cases of failure of improvement or unpredicted improvements, clinicians must refine their model or theory either by gathering more data if that option is available or trying to figure out what happened with knowledgeable colleagues in case conferences or other settings where post mortems can be done or where "pathology" can be examined in an objective detached manner.

Thus building theoretical models of health and testing them against the observed responses to interventions is one way of conceptualizing the validation process in clinical work. Ethnographers use the same method to check their understanding of what may be going on and whether they have properly understood it, but for ethnographers this represents more of an intermediate validation step, whereas for clinicians it is often the only form of ultimate validation available. It is for this reason, perhaps, that the clinical method is sometimes viewed as "less scientific" than the methods that ultimately hinge on replication. In the effort to increase their scientific status, clinicians often resort to replication attempts by bringing in colleagues to view the same situation, or working in front of one-way mirrors with colleagues or supervisors watching (if and when that is possible from the client perspective). But if the assumption is correct that clinicians by definition intervene in systems and, thereby, change the system, we need a fundamentally different way of assessing the validity of such intervention. Simply imposing the traditional scientific criteria will always find clinical data wanting. Yet given the amount of faith we apparently put in data obtained first hand in this manner, there must be a way to legitimize such data. I believe that the ability to predict the outcomes of interventions is the best direction to pursue.

Clinical Data as a Source of Better Theory

As shown above, the clinician often may have a harder time validating specific findings than the ethnographer, but that may not ultimately be the most important scientific aspect of the clinical perspective anyway. Instead there is the possibility that the best use of clinical data is in the construction of variables and theoretical models. The clinician learns about some of the most fundamental dynamics that operate in an organization, and it is often very clear, even though not provable, what those dynamics are.

For example, we have known for a long time that power and authority were important variables in organization theory, yet have produced very little real insight into the dynamics of power because we have not had access to information about what goes on at the power centers of organizations. Since senior executives are some of the most frequent users of consulting services, it would seem that it is the consultants who would "know" most about how power is used and how it operates. Yet we have remarkably little theory that takes into account the kind of information that consultants obtain.

On the other hand, when we do get insights into this level from books such as *The Neurotic Organization* (Kets de Vries & Miller, 1984) or from the early Tavistock studies, we immediately recognize the importance of the findings though they are based on limited case material. My hypothesis is that we treat those findings as very important because they illuminate theoretically large areas where previously we had only unexplained anomalies.

If the clinician happens to be at the right place at the right time when some critical organizational event takes place involving key actors in the organizational drama, one has the basis for theory construction to be validated with other case materials and ethnographic information. For example, we knew from clinical data and biographical information that general managers' jobs were highly varied, fragmented, and complex, but we did not finally accept this as "fact" until it was confirmed by more ethnographic data from the Mintzberg (1973), Kotter (1982), and Stewart (1967, 1976) studies. My point is that we "knew" long before their research confirmed these insights what general managers did.

To me the power of clinical work such as that carried out by Argyris et al. (1985) under the label of "action science," by Levinson (1972), by Zaleznik and Kets de Vries (1975), and the many practitioners of organization development (e.g., Beckhard & Harris, 1977) is that such work provides better variables and better understanding of system dynamics than other research methods and thus must be utilized more in building useful and parsimonious theory.

A very similar argument can, of course, be made for ethnographic research. I have not reviewed that argument because it has been widely accepted that ethnographies reveal dynamics of human systems and help us to build better theory. The clinical perspective needs to be brought together with the ethnographic because the two perspectives focus us on different aspects of human systems.

Summary and Conclusions

I have tried to show that clinicians and ethnographers have different priorities in how they gather and validate their information, stemming from the different goals and psychological contracts they have with members of the organization. For the ethnographer, replication is a primary criterion, but prediction of outcomes is relatively secondary. For the clinician, it is predicting the consequences of given interventions that is a primary criterion while replication is typically not possible anyway in a dynamic system.

The clinical method as a way of gathering credible organizational data typically is regarded as less scientific because it does not rely on the traditional scientific criteria or paradigms, particularly those dealing with quantification and the control of experimental variables. Prediction is a valid criterion but the clinician can predict only in limited areas and cannot generate control groups. Often the crucial prediction cannot be tested because the clinician would be unwilling to make the intervention that would produce the test.

Nevertheless clinical work produces deep insight into many aspects of organizational dynamics, so we must find ways of giving more visibility and credence to such insights. It is particularly important to develop the scientific status of clinical insight because clinicians are often asked to help higher-level people in organizations and thus get insight into power dynamics and the workings of hierarchies that are difficult for ethnographers and any other categories of organizational scientists to obtain. Such information is critical to the building of better variables and theories in our field.

4. PROFESSIONAL AND ETHICAL ISSUES IN CLINICAL VERSUS ETHNOGRAPHIC WORK

How Should the Investigator Be Trained to Conduct Inquiry?

The contrast between clinicians and ethnographers clearly shows up when we examine the typical training programs they undergo. The clinician is typically trained in theories that focus on models of pathology and health, effectiveness, coping, dynamics, and intervention. Most often these come from psychiatry, clinical psychology, applied psychology, sociology or anthropology, organization development, social work, and other disciplines that focus on changing and improving human systems.

The ethnographer, in contrast, is typically trained in theories that emphasize description, how total social systems work, often explicitly rejecting normative theories of how they should work. Such theories more often come from sociology, anthropology, political science, and social psychology. Notice that some of the same disciplines are involved in both fields, but that in those disciplines the distinction between the pure and the applied wings are often quite significant in how they define the training requirements for their graduates.

Both ethnographers and clinicians have to learn to observe, to develop relationships with clients and subjects, to listen attentively, to elicit information in conversations and interviews, and to use structured devices for gathering information. But these devices are totally different in the two models reflecting the different goals that have been articulated above. Thus the clinician may use a variety of diagnostic devices to elicit data about areas of health and pathology, whereas the ethnographer would use something more akin to the camera, devices that just record what is going on with a minimum of prior bias on what should be focused on. The ethnographic paradigm is, of course, undergoing radical change itself toward more of an interpretive view that acknowledges the importance of the observer both as a filter and as an interpreter of what is going on (Van Maanen, 1987).

Both have to do "fieldwork" but the clinician is likely to get his training in contexts where people with problems are getting some form of treatment or education, whereas the ethnographer learns to live among the "natives" he or she is supposed to study. For the organizational clinician, the applied training ground is often human relations workshops where sensitivity training and other activities are used to improve the insight and skill of participants through a variety of experiential exercises and activities with the student clinician in a coaching helping role (Schein & Bennis, 1965).

Such practical experience in a context where people have paid to come for education, training, and therapy are essential components of the training of clinicians. They learn there how to establish helping relationships, how to give clients a feeling that it is in the client's best interest to continue the relationship. Helping theory and consultation theory thus become central learning foci, and the practice of helping becomes a primary skill. It is these particular skills that may be focused on less in the training of the ethnographer.

Ethnographers also want the relationship to continue so that data can continue to be elicited, but being seen as helpful is not the primary goal. More likely the goal is to be seen as minimally obtrusive, to be accepted comfortably so that one will be invited to participate in more and more activities of the group being studied. Fieldwork for the ethnographer, therefore, is to live with the group and learn as much as possible how their world looks to them, to become an observing participant or participant observer.

Clinicians can afford to be confrontive in various ways so long as they are seen as helpful; ethnographers have to be more careful with confrontation lest they be seen as a nuisance. In fact, ethnographers may have the opposite problem of learning how to accept a variety of confrontive behaviors from their subjects as the subjects decide to test them to discover how trustworthy they are and how sincere their interest is in their organization. Ethnographers may be subjected to hazing and other forms of tests that clinicians would not have to participate in if they chose not to.

Clinicians have to learn to exercise the responsibility that goes with the authority of the helping role. The psychological contract puts clinicians into a position of power that provides a certain license to dispense advice and prescription. The skill of exercising that power responsibly on behalf of the client is central to learning the clinical method.

Ethnographers do not have such power attributed to them in the first place, hence they do not have to learn this particular skill, but ethnographers do have to learn how to decipher very quickly what kinds of things subjects do attribute to them, what power they are granted, so that they do not unwittingly offend and undermine their ability to remain in the organization. As was mentioned above, they are likely to be seen as knowing a great deal about organizations and to have extraordinary levels of insight by virtue of their academic affiliations. They may therefore be asked for all sorts of advice and be seen as unhelpful and aloof if they refuse to comment.

The formal training process of the clinician does or at least should involve a Masters (i.e., social work) or Ph.D.-level academic training, an internship, some sort of "residency" or practice under supervision, and some sort of credentialing process by both the training institution and the community in the form of being "licensed" to practice. The field in which this process is least developed and, therefore, most problematic is in consulting, especially organizational development and process consultation. In order to be able to take the clinical perspective responsibly consultants should, therefore, have the equivalent training to the other clinical fields mentioned.

The training process for the ethnographer is also typically a Ph.D.-level academic program involving a year or more of fieldwork, practice in gathering, analyzing, and describing data obtained in the field, a thesis, publications in relevant scientific journals, and ultimately some kind of credentialing as a researcher/scholar. Such credentialing is typically the granting of tenure by a relevant academic institution, a process that heavily involves academic peers but rarely the community. It is the skills of data gathering and reporting that are central to this process, not typically the skills of establishing helping relationships with clients. Perhaps another way of saying this to sharpen the distinction is to note that clinicians have to learn to communicate with their potential and actual clients, while ethnographers have to learn to communicate with their subjects and their scientific/academic colleagues. For the clinician to learn to translate insights obtained in the field into scientifically valid useful information is a secondary skill, just as for the ethnographer to learn to help his or her subjects is a secondary skill. It is this secondary learning for each type that is the real challenge because in organizational work the two roles so often come to blend into each other.

How Clinicians and Ethnographers Are Alike

Shared role dilemmas. Both clinicians and ethnographers are limited in what topics they can focus on by what the clients or subjects attribute to them based on their sex, age, formal status, nationality, color, and any other fairly visible attribute. For example, very young clinicians or ethnographers will not get much access to higher levels of organizations where older and more powerful members reside, in part because those members will assume that the younger person would not understand the issues they deal with anyway. Women will be excluded from some areas assumed to be strictly male domains, and men will be excluded from some areas assumed to be strictly female domains.

The clinician or researcher from a prestigious institution or with prestigious personal credentials will often be able to learn more and be opened up to more than someone with lesser credentials. Someone of another nationality or ethnic group may not be told things because it would be assumed that he or she "would not understand." Such dilemmas can ultimately be overcome only by having teams of researchers who represent a spectrum of role attributes working in organizations and pooling their insights.

Shared commitment to scientific objectivity. Both clinicians and ethnographers have a commitment to scientific objectivity and are trained in how to maintain such objectivity. That implies the ability to remain detached even when in the midst of helping or participating, and the ability to process observations in a detached scientific manner. Though the theoretical premises may be very different, as noted above, both methods imply a basic commitment to a scientific model in the broad sense.

If clients or subjects lie, dissemble, hide data, or in other ways distort reality, both clinicians and ethnographers are trained in how to spot such distortions and how to correct for them. The methods used for correction, cross-checking, and validating are different, but the commitment to validity is shared.

Shared capacity to operate backstage. Both clinicians and ethnographers are likely to become exposed to information that may be emotionally uncomfortable, yet have to continue to function in their role. They are permitted, even invited, backstage and what is often labeled "dirty linen" is likely to be exposed to them. They must not react with shock or disapproval no matter how dirty the linen, and they must display professional responsibility in not misusing the information thus obtained.

From an emotional point of view, this often means that the only people with whom one can share such information are professional colleagues. One cannot engage in organizational gossip, and one cannot use "insider" information for personal gain. This often means a frustrating process of having to sit on information that cannot be shared with anyone and that can never be published because even if disguised it could be harmful to the client or subject.

I suspect that much of the impatience clinicians and ethnographers experience with respect to organizational research done in more traditional ways is that backstage realities that inform such research cannot really be brought into the academic debate, yet the researcher knows that what is published is so incomplete as to be virtually useless. For example, I have little faith in research on organization structure variables done with questionnaires to senior executives because I have seen how such executives, on the one hand, describe their organization as highly decentralized, while listening to them tell me, on the other hand, how they have to control daily various kinds of activities to ensure that lower-level executives do the right things. They believe they are decentralized and are sincere in their answer to the question, but they behave in a manner that would lead to a different rating if it were made on clinical or ethnographic information.

Some examples of sensitive information. I was involved, some years ago, with a company in which the primary client wanted help in developing a program to educate the person who would become president on how to be a better manager. The client was a vice president, an older man who had foreseen the succession problem and feared that unless the incumbent really developed some skills in the near future the company would suffer.

Working out a seminar program, individual counseling sessions, and various kinds of projects in which the incumbent president could become involved without in any way leaking the real purpose of all of these programs became quite a difficult job of social engineering. The more I became involved, the more I learned about the real "weaknesses" of the future president and the more difficult it became to create situations that would serve to develop this person.

The politics that occurred around the top management team were constant and pervasive and one could not in any way predict how the situation would evolve. Yet even two levels down in the organization it was business as usual and various kinds of surveys done in the organization revealed neither knowledge of nor concern about any of these matters.

I learned from this how unstable organizational processes really are, in that I knew what was ahead as this person would take office a year hence, yet could not in any way reveal to others who would be affected what kinds of changes would occur.

Another example involves misattribution of causality. A large company about which many cases have been written developed a particular strategic thrust as a result of some systematic exercises in strategic analysis. The published information implies that the choice of strategy was the result of a particular kind of analysis of the products and markets, yet I knew from working with the organization near the top that the founder of the organization had a personal bias toward that particular strategy and ensured that it would be implemented by putting into the key managerial positions at the top of the organization only people who were known to support that strategy. The exercise was after the fact. The cause of the strategic thrust was the founder's behind-the-scenes manipulation.

A related example illustrates incompleteness of information. A company that is heavily dependent upon its technical resources is known to have developed an effective dual career ladder for its scientists and engineers. Much has been written about the grades and salary levels and how well administered the system is, putting the focus on the principle that if the incentives are suitable the dual ladder will work.

What I learned from working with this organization in a clinical role is that the scientists in the organization really believed in the dual ladder for quite different reasons. First of all, they trusted the president of the organization to back it because he had shown strong commitment to scientists throughout the history of the company. The good incentives in the structure resulted directly from his personally mandating it.

Second, there were known but little talked about cases of scientists going into management who were failing as managers but who were seen as good technical resources. Such people were encouraged to leave management without feeling personally disgraced and picked up on the ladder. But, even more important, there were cases of failed managers who were not any longer seen as technical resources who were *not* allowed to take slots on the technical ladder, and it was those incidents that really convinced young scientists that the technical ladder was "for real," not just a dumping ground or show piece for a few token scientists.

Finally, a case of how policy really works was revealed in the Action Co. many years ago. One critical assumption in the culture of the Action Co. was that employees should always think for themselves and "do the *right* thing," not necessarily the thing that the boss dictated. The Corporate Personnel Office had issued a policy that sales managers were not to drive better cars than salesmen because the company was aggressively egalitarian. I had learned that in several overseas offices this policy was regarded as suicidal because in those countries status symbols mattered a great deal and managers needed better cars. I was asked by some of them to try to get the policy altered when I next met with the corporate personnel group.

My request was greeted with laughter, and my request for an explanation of the laughter was followed by the clear statement that those sales offices should just have gone out and bought the cars. The policy was there as a principle, not as a constraint. Had I not attended that particular meeting, I would never have found out what the attitude of senior management toward their own policies really was, and would have possibly drawn some erroneous conclusions about what was going on in this company.

Material of this kind can be revealed anonymously and years after it really matters, but is extremely difficult to use in a scientific way when one first confronts it. This leads to the final issue to be discussed.

Some Ethical Dilemmas
in Fieldwork with Human Systems

Data gathering as intervention. In contrasting clinicians with ethnographers I have been able to sharpen some points, but some others have yet to be confronted. Specifically, I have argued that both types have been *trained* to be careful with respect to their clients or subjects, to be helpful and/or to be as minimally disturbing to the system as possible. These contrasts in how to be responsible come out more clearly when we compare both models with some other approaches to working with organizations that are popular today under the broad umbrella of organization studies.

Many organizational researchers who have not obtained either clinical or ethnographic training may be doing unknown amounts of damage to the systems that they study, either by intervening harmfully or disturbing the system in unknown and potentially destructive ways. Specifically, I am referring to those researchers who do organizational surveys or who obtain data with interviews without in any way being concerned about being helpful or unobtrusive. Usually such methods simply assume incorrectly that one can obtain data without influencing and/or disturbing the system. I think that both clinicians and ethnographers would agree that this represents a degree of irresponsibility that needs to be addressed explicitly.

From the clinical point of view, it is not possible to interact with another human being or group without influencing them to some degree. If I send some persons a questionnaire, I have already communicated to them that they are on some list (something they may have been unaware of) and the questions I ask will raise questions and issues in their mind that they may never have thought of before. If they become aware that others also received the questionnaire, they may discuss it and compare answers, and thus discover similarities and differences among themselves that they were not previously aware of.

For example, in an attitude survey run by a company several employees may discover that they have a common dislike of their boss, something that they had not revealed to each other before, and may then decide to collude against their boss. Or the questions may deal with various organizational policies that the employees never thought about, but in answering questions about those policies they become interested and develop feelings toward them.

Or the participants in the research assume that by virtue of providing data to a researcher they will obtain some feedback on their own situation or someone else will obtain feedback and fix problems that may have been revealed in the data. If nothing happens as a result of the research, morale may decline and management may be blamed for inaction without realizing why any of this is happening.

All such influences operate even more strongly when one interviews subjects. I have argued elsewhere in discussing consultation models that one of the most powerful tools consultants have for influencing the client's thinking is the kinds of questions they ask, because those questions can direct the client's thinking into specific areas and even suggest specific solutions or answers (Schein, 1969, 1987). The same is true for researchers, except that researchers are often not concerned about their impact on the subject and hence will act irresponsibly to an unknown degree in choosing their questions.

The major implication of this line of reasoning is that *all* researchers who deal with human systems must have some degree of clinical training, specifically training around client responsibility and the consequences of data-gathering interventions. The logic of scientific inquiry into organizations must somehow take into account that inquiry itself is an intervention that has implications not only for data validity, but, more important, for the relationship with the people in the organization.

We have seen how "society" has reacted to some of the perceived irresponsibility that has accompanied experimentation with human subjects in psychology. Following the guidelines set up by the Department of Health, Education, and Welfare, and adopted by many universities, subjects are now asked to give consent and institutions have set up all kinds of mechanisms to monitor researchers to ensure that such consent is given. From my point of view, this solution misses the point altogether in assuming that the subject is capable of assessing the consequences of something he or she has not yet experienced. From a clinical action research perspective, the responsibility must reside in the researcher because only the researcher really knows from past experience what the consequences of given interventions will be.

Instead of attempting to monitor research and have unwitting subjects sign consent forms, we need to build into our academic training much more of a clinical point of view so that the researcher knows from the outset how research influences subjects and organizations, and has the sense of responsibility to only do research that can be judged to be helpful and benign.

We must stop kidding ourselves that traditional organizational research based on researchers going into organizations to gather data by counting, surveying, or interviewing is either valid or harmless. There is a real possibility that such research not only harms members of the organization but also produces superficial and incorrect insights into what happens in organizations.

The choice between the clinical and the ethnographic is itself an important choice, but I would argue for either of those methods over most of the ones that have traditionally been used in the field of "organization behavior" and on which most of our organizational "science" has so far been built.

Obligations with respect to feedback and publication. In most traditional research projects the simplistic assumption is made that if the researcher provides some feedback and debriefing to the subject, whatever harm may have been done during the research or inquiry process can now be explained and undone. So if we obligate ourselves to give feedback, we can proceed. Not so, from the clinical perspective.

Many things that the researcher might "feed back" would produce more harm in making visible something that the organization may have been committed to keeping implicit. If an organization agrees to a survey and it is discovered that most of the employees have a given attitude toward something, the surfacing of that information through a feedback process can be devastating to the organization. Similarly, if I interview an employee as part of a research project and he or she asks me how their opinions compare to those of others I have heard, I cannot simply say whatever I know without considering the implications for the person who asked the question. What if he or she is completely alone in their opinion?

What we have forgotten in much of the usage of the term "providing feedback," is that feedback is "information relevant to progress toward some goal." In the clinical situation, the goals are the client's in terms of where they are trying to get, and those goals determine for the clinician when, how, and what to say that may be useful to the client in relation to his or her goals. In the research situation, especially in the ethnographic one, if the subject asks "What have you found out about us so far?" what is missing is knowledge of the subject's goals. Hence the researcher has no way of knowing what the potential impact of any given answer will be.

The only way out of this dilemma is to take a clinical stance toward it in the first place and not to promise any feedback except in relation to goals that the subject may be willing to articulate. If the persons being observed or interviewed say that they have always wondered about how to improve their supervisory process, then ethnographers, if they are willing, can say that as they observe they can note incidents relative to the supervisory process and at some future time meet with them to discuss it. However, they have to guide what they say by the clinical criteria of being helpful; they cannot simply spill whatever may have been observed in an uncritical fashion.

The other dilemma that requires some clinical skills is how to decide to whom to give what data. The standard survey technique in organizations almost automatically assumes that if top management pays for the survey they get the first crack at seeing what the data showed. They can then give to each department the relevant data to be discussed and acted upon. The comparable situation for the ethnographer might be if the senior management of the organization invited him or her to give an overview presentation of what he or she had found in their fieldwork before anyone else had seen the data.

From a clinical perspective, this could be harmful, and almost certainly will not be helpful. Instead, what would make much more sense is to negotiate at the outset that any information obtained from any particular group or department in the organization will be fed back to that group prior to anyone else seeing that information. The group still "owns" the information and has a right to decide what to do about it. If the group sees the information first it can decide how to correct, elaborate, and otherwise embellish the information, thus providing some validation and some new information. If the information contains material potentially harmful to the group it can suppress this information before it reaches higher levels. The researcher should never be in the position of leaking potentially harmful information from one group in the organization to another.

In the clinical context where problem solving and organization improvement is the issue, giving each group feedback about itself has additional advantages. It permits the group to sort out those elements of what it has reported that it can work on itself and pass on to higher levels only those problems that need higher-level attention. This reduces dependency on higher management levels, motivates problem solving at those levels where the problems exist, and empowers the group to act on its own behalf. When surveys are initially fed back to top management, one typically sees the lower-level groups becoming passive and dependent, wondering what management will now do with all the information and gripes that have been revealed.

What of the special case of giving to the organization whatever the ethnographer has finally written up as his or her analysis in order to check its validity or simply as a courtesy or to complete the "contract?" Or, if the clinician has decided that a given case merits publication, what are the pros and cons of giving it to the client prior to publication for possible editing if potentially harmful things have been said from the client's point of view?

Both of these are tough cases. Ethnographers are committed to getting a publication out of their research, so they usually negotiate in the first place the right to publish what they write, but may agree to let the subject edit it. Clinicians cannot extract such a promise from a client without violating their basic obligation that they are providing help for a fee. If something of scientific value comes out of the cases, they must totally disguise them, be willing to check them with the subject, and potentially be willing not to publish them.

In any case, the clinical view would argue that the real name of the organizational client must never be used because there is no way of telling ahead of time where a given organization will be vulnerable and in what way published material about it could be harmful. Even if the organization has cleared the material, I have seen examples where identified cases have led years later to organizational "harm."

For example, a company that was studied in the 1970s when it was young and entrepreneurial was written up to show how hard driving and aggressive it was. That same company in the 1980s was much larger and had changed its style substantially, but students who read the earlier case in a strategy course revealed that they did not even sign up for interviews with the recruiter from the company because of the impression they formed of it in the case description.

When we publish to fulfill our own scientific needs, we must recognize that we may be compromising the needs of the organization that provided the information. In training organizational researchers we must, therefore, make them aware of the importance of taking a clinical stance toward their subjects before rushing into a project.

The ethical dilemmas of research with humans and human organizations are pervasive and difficult. There are no easy answers to be found, no quick resolutions. But one can acknowledge that the dilemmas are there and ask our students, the organizational researchers of the future, to take a hard look at them and face them. In this sense, my ultimate argument is that all research on humans must be informed to some degree by a clinical point of view, and that our academic training programs must include some material on the clinical method and the issues that it raises.

The Clinical Perspective in Summary

The essence of the clinical perspective can be summarized best in the following several points:

(1) The process is client initiated.
(2) The inquiry is client and problem centered.
(3) The inquiry is oriented toward pathology and health.
(4) The process involves exchange of services for fees.
(5) Data come from client needs and perspectives.
(6) Inquiry comes from the clinician's theory of health.
(7) Data are deep but not broad.
(8) Data involve matters that must be kept confidential.
(9) Data are validated through predicting responses to interventions.
(10) Data are analyzed in case conferences, through sharing with colleagues.
(11) The ethical/legal responsibility is to avoid malpractice.
(12) Training is focused on helping skills and supported by an internship.
(13) Scientific results are secondary to helping.
(14) Clinical data are one valid basis for doing organizational research.
(15) Clinical research may be the best way to learn about what goes on in the power centers of organizations.

In concluding this analysis I would like to reiterate that a combination of clinical and ethnographic research done by a team representing different ages, sexes, roles, and statuses is to me the most promising avenue for unraveling the mysteries of organizational life. I hope our organizational science can incorporate, indeed encourage, such a direction.

A Personal Note

In the first chapter I related our MIT experience in starting a clinical seminar. I learned in that seminar and have observed in subsequent academic seminars how deeply committed we seem to be in academia to intellectual debate. However, as I reflect back on that seminar, what struck me was how low the quality of the debate really was because none of us were very good at listening.

I learned to listen during my clinical training. In sitting for hours on end in training groups and during interviews in which people talked about the problems they wanted to work on, I learned personally how hard it is to concentrate on someone else when one's own head is so full of one's own brilliant insights. One of the most powerful exercises we did in those workshops was called "helping trios" where one person stated a problem, one person was a helper, and one person was a silent observer. It was almost totally predictable that the observer would see the helper not really listening and consequently giving inappropriate advice or making premature judgments. We then would rotate the roles and keep going until each of us had been in each role.

In our organizational psychology classes we use an exercise that requires group members during a discussion to restate what the previous speaker had said, to that person's satisfaction, before they can make their own point. Most groups angrily abandon the exercise after 10 to 15 minutes, but by then the point has been made.

In our clinical seminar we learned to listen once we had a videotape of ourselves and could see how we jumped in, overrode others, fought for our points of view, and rarely listened. In our seminar we debated hard, but was it a debate or a serial process of each of us broadcasting our own position in the hope that it was so clear and well stated that it would override the barriers of the nonlisteners? And why were we so defensive about the interpretation that intellectual discourse is intrinsically an aggressive process in which there are winners and losers? Once we saw on tape how we managed ourselves, insight grew and defensiveness declined.

If we are to introduce any clinical training into our programs, it seems to me we have to come to terms with the aggressiveness and the need to broadcast instead of listen. The intellectual enterprise is a tough one, so being strong and aggressive is, no doubt, a necessity and probably a virtue. But if I am at all right about organizational research, we have to learn how to leave the aggressive nonlistening self at the university, and go into organizations with humility, curiosity, and enormously well-developed listening skills. Can we do it?

REFERENCES

Argyris, C., Putnam, R., & Smith, D. M. (1985). *Action science*. San Francisco: Jossey-Bass.

Barley, S. R. (1984a). *The professional, the semi-professional, and the machine: The social implications of computer based imaging in radiology*. Unpublished Doctoral Dissertation, MIT, Sloan School of Management, Cambridge.

Barley, S. R. (1984b). *Technology as an occasion for structuration: Observations on CT scanners and the social order of radiology departments*. Cambridge, MA: MIT, Sloan School of Management.

Beckhard, R., & Harris, R. (1977). *Organizational transitions: Managing complex change*. Reading, MA: Addison-Wesley.

Bennis, W. G. (1962). Toward a "truly" scientific management: The concept of organizational health. *Industrial Management Review (MIT), 4*(1), 1-27.

Geertz, C. (1973). *The interpretation of cultures*. New York: Basic Books.

Goffman, E. (1959). *The presentation of self in everyday life*. New York: Doubleday.

Kets de Vries, M.F.R., & Miller, D. (1984). *The neurotic organization*. San Francisco: Jossey-Bass.

Kotter, J. P. (1982). *The general managers*. New York: Free Press.

Levinson, H. (1972). *Organizational diagnosis*. Cambridge, MA: Harvard University Press.

Lewin, K. (Ed.). (1948). *Resolving social conflicts*. New York: Harper & Row.

Lippitt, R., Watson, J., & Westley, B. (1958). *Dynamics of planned change*. New York: Harcourt Brace Jovanovich.

McGregor, D. M. (1960). *The human side of enterprise*. New York: McGraw-Hill.

Mintzberg, H. (1973). *The nature of managerial work*. New York: Harper & Row.

Rice, A. K. (1963). *The enterprise and its environment*. London: Tavistock.

Schein, E. H. (1956). The Chinese indoctrination program for prisoners of war. *Psychiatry, 19*, 149-172.

Schein, E. H. (1961). *Coercive persuasion*. New York: Norton.

Schein, E. H. (1966). The problem of moral education for the business manager. *Industrial Management Review, 8*, 3-14.

Schein, E. H. (1969). *Process consultation*. Reading, MA: Addison-Wesley.

Schein, E. H. (1972). *Professional education: Some new directions*. New York: McGraw-Hill.

Schein, E. H. (1980). *Organizational psychology* (3rd ed.). Englewood Cliffs, NJ: Prentice-Hall.

Schein, E. H. (1985). *Organizational culture and leadership*. San Francisco: Jossey-Bass.

Schein, E. H. (1987). *Process consultation* (Vol. 2). Reading, MA: Addison-Wesley.

Schein, E. H., & Bennis, W. G. (1965). *Personal and organizational change through group methods*. New York: John Wiley.

Stewart, R. (1967). *Managers and their jobs.* New York: Macmillan.

Stewart, R. (1976). *Contrasts in management.* New York: McGraw-Hill.

Trist, E. L., Higgin, G. W., Murray, H., & Pollock, A. B. (1963). *Organizational choice.* London: Tavistock.

Van Maanen, J. (in press) *Tales of the field.* Chicago: University of Chicago Press.

Zaleznik, A., & Kets de Vries, M.F.R. (1975). *Power and the corporate mind.* Boston: Houghton Mifflin.

ABOUT THE AUTHOR

Edgar H. Schein received his undergraduate education from the University of Chicago and Stanford University. He received a Ph.D. in Social Psychology from Harvard University's Social Relations Department in 1952. After four years as a Research Psychologist and Head of the Social Psychology Research Section of the Walter Reed Army Institute of Research, he joined the faculty of the Sloan School of Management, MIT, where he became a Professor in 1964. He was Chairman of the Organization Studies Group from 1972 to 1982. Schein has worked primarily as a social psychologist concentrating on the relationship between the individual and the organization. He is especially interested in how organizations influence individual behavior, attitudes, and beliefs, and has published extensively on the topic of organizational socialization, management development, career dynamics, and, most recently, organizational culture. He is the author of *Organizational Psychology*, now in its third edition, one of the first books to define that field. Other books are *Coercive Persuasion, Interpersonal Dynamics, Professional Education: Some New Directions, Process Consultation, Career Dynamics, Personal and Organizational Change Through Group Methods,* and, most recently, *Organizational Culture and Leadership.* Schein has worked as an experimental social psychologist, as a clinician, and has done extensive consulting with organizations. He was trained at Harvard in a broad interdisciplinary program that included anthropology. In this book he attempts to clarify some of these perspectives by showing how they differ.